HOW TO READ A FINANCIAL REPORT

HOW TO READ A

WRINGING VITAL SIGNS OUT OF

Fourth Edition

JOHN WILEY & SONS, INC.

NEW YORK   CHICHESTER   BRISBANE

FINANCIAL REPORT

THE NUMBERS

JOHN A. TRACY, Ph.D., CPA

TORONTO   SINGAPORE

Library of Congress Cataloging in Publication Data

Tracy, John A.
   How to read a financial report: wringing vital signs out of the numbers/John A. Tracy.—4th ed.
      p. cm.
   Includes index.
   ISBN 0–471–59390–7 (cloth)—ISBN 0–471–59391–5 (pbk.)
   1. Financial statements.   I. Title.
HF5681.B2T733   1994
657'.3—dc20   93-23783
                                    CIP

Printed in the United States of America
10 9 8 7 6 5 4 3 2

PREFACE TO THE FOURTH EDITION

When I started this book I had no grandchildren; today I have five. Jimmy Carter was President; today Bill Clinton sits in the White House. The problems, issues, and hot spots of financial reporting certainly have changed since the late 1970s.

This new edition offers several improvements:

♦ the centerpiece exhibit is all new; this basic example, which is used throughout the book, now includes a two-year, comparative balance sheet that helps to explain the cash flow statement much better.

♦ businesses did not adopt the so-called direct format for the Cash Flow Statement, so the chapter in the previous edition that explained this format has been dropped.

♦ a very significant new financial reporting standard was mandated in late 1990 concerning accounting for post-retirement health care and medical benefits; this development is the core of a new chapter that explores the making and changing of financial reporting rules (Chapter 20).

Without sounding too immodest, I hope, the basic content and approach of the book remains the same; it has proven very successful. "If it ain't broke, don't fix it." So, I have been careful in making changes. I have updated the material where necessary, of course. Otherwise, I have tried not to sharpen the editing blue pencil too often.

I wish to thank the many readers who have taken the time to call or write. I want to thank particularly my students at the University of Colorado who have made many helpful suggestions. Nothing is so satisfying as to hear that the book has helped someone to make better sense of financial statements.

As before, I want to express my deepest appreciation to Gordon Laing, the first editor on the book, for his guidance, encouragement, and friendship. Although now retired he takes as much pride of accomplishment in the book as I do, as well he should. Gordon, you old reprobate, I couldn't have done it without you.

JOHN A. TRACY

Boulder, Colorado
March 1993

CONTENTS

1

STARTING WITH CASH FLOWS

Importance of Cash Flows:
A Cash Flow Summary for the Business

Business managers, lenders, and investors are, quite rightly, very concerned with cash flows. Cash inflows and outflows are the heartbeat of any business. So let's start here. For our example we'll use a middle-size business that has completed several years of operations. It is making a profit and is in reasonably good financial condition.

A summary of the company's cash receipts and cash disbursements for the most recent year of business is given in Exhibit A. Exhibit A shows three sources of cash receipts and six uses (disbursements) of cash during the year. Each source and use should be fairly familiar, so the following description of the company's activities is very brief:

♦ The company received money from the sale of products to its customers. Also, the company borrowed money on interest-bearing notes, and stockholders invested money in the corporation.

♦ The company paid out money for the purchase of products sold to its customers, and also paid out money for operating expenses, as well as for interest and income tax expenses. The company bought and paid for building improvements, machines and equipment, as well as office furniture. Last, the business paid cash dividends to its stockholders during the year.

EXHIBIT A - SUMMARY OF CASH RECEIPTS AND DISBURSEMENTS FOR YEAR

Cash Receipts

From customers for products sold to them	$5,922,636	
From borrowing on interest-bearing notes	125,000	
From issuing new capital stock shares in the corporation	100,000	
Total cash receipts during year		$6,147,636

Cash Disbursements

For purchases of products that were sold or are being held for sale	$4,030,205	
For many different expenses of operating the business	1,484,099	
For interest on notes payable	74,231	
For income tax, some of which was due on last year's taxable income	132,218	
For building improvements, new machinery, and new equipment that will last several years	389,400	
For cash distributions to stockholders from the net income (profit) earned by the business for the year, which are called dividends	93,750	
Total cash disbursements during year		$6,203,903
Net Decrease In Cash During Year		($ 56,267)

What Does the Summary of Cash Flows NOT Tell You?

What does Exhibit A tell you? One thing it tells you is that cash, that all-important lubricant of business activity, decreased $56,267 during the year. Disbursements exceeded receipts by this amount for the entire year.

But what does Exhibit A *not* tell you that you absolutely need to know? The two most important things that the cash summary does not tell you are:

1. The *profit* for the year.

2. The *financial condition* or position of the business at the end of the year.

Why doesn't Exhibit A tell you the profit earned during the year? Profit is the total revenue (gross proceeds) from sale of products to customers less all expenses of making the sales and operating the business. You can't count money borrowed or money invested by stockholders as sales revenue. Certainly you don't earn profit by borrowing money that has to be repaid later, or by stockholders investing capital in the business.

So the first step is to distinguish between two quite different sources of cash: (a) the cash received from sales revenue, and (b) the cash received from borrowing and stockholders' investments.

Next, we have to ask whether all the cash disbursements during the year are for expenses that should be deducted from sales revenue to determine profit. The first four disbursements in Exhibit A are certainly expense related. But the fifth disbursement is far too much to charge off entirely against sales revenue for the year. These expenditures for building improvements, machines, equipment, and furniture are *long-term* investments. These resources are used over several years. To deduct all their cost in the year of purchase would be very misleading for profit measurement.

Also, cash dividends are a distribution of profit and not an expense to deduct against sales revenue. In other words, dividends are **after** profit. Indeed, the company first has to know whether or not it earned a profit to pay dividends from.

Profit Cannot Be Measured by Cash Flows

Hardly ever are cash flows during a certain period the correct amounts to measure profit (or loss) for that period. To start with, this company, like the vast majority of businesses, sells its products *on credit*. At the end of the year, this company has *receivables* from sales made to its customers during the last part of the year. These receivables will be collected (in cash) during the early part of next year.

So the cash received during the year from customers is not total sales revenue for the year. The amount of receivables at year-end has to be added to the cash received. And, the cash received from sales made last year should be deducted.

Cash disbursements are *not* the correct amounts for measuring expenses. Like sales revenue, the cash amount is not the whole story. The company paid out $4,030,205 for purchases of products during the year (see Exhibit A). At year-end, however, many products are still on hand in *inventory*. In other words, some of the products bought during the year have not yet been sold by the end of the year. Only the cost of products sold and delivered to customers during the year should be deducted as expense from sales revenue to measure profit.

Furthermore, some of its year-end inventory had not yet been paid for at year-end. The company buys its products on credit and takes some time before paying its bills. So the company has a *liability* at year-end for these recent purchases.

The cash payments during the year for operating expenses, as well as for interest and income tax expenses, are *not* the correct amounts to deduct from sales revenue to measure profit for the year. The company also has *liabilities* at the end of the year for these expenses. The cash disbursement amounts shown in Exhibit A do not include the additional amounts of these expenses that are unpaid at the end of the year.

The main point is this: Cash flows are *not* the correct amounts needed to determine profit for a period of time. Cash flows do not include the complete sales revenue and expense activities for the period. A complete accounting is necessary to measure profit.

This "complete accounting" is known as the *accrual basis*. Accrual basis accounting records the receivables from making sales on credit, and also records the liabilities for unpaid expenses, in order to determine the correct profit measure for the period.

Accrual basis accounting is also necessary to get a complete look at the company's assets other than cash, as well as its liabilities and other sources of capital.

Cash Flows Do Not Reveal Financial Condition

The cash receipts and disbursements summary for the year (Exhibit A) does not reveal the financial condition of the company. The business manager certainly needs to know the asset situation of the company; that is, how much receivables, inventory, and other assets the company has. Also, the manager needs to know the amounts of the company's liabilities. The manager has the responsibility of keeping the company in a position to pay its liabilities when they come due. And the manager has to know whether the assets are too large (or too small) relative to the sales volume of the company. Lenders and investors are also very interested in the same things.

In short, managers, lenders, and investors all need a summary report of the financial condition (assets, liabilities, etc.) of a business. And they need a correct profit performance report, which sums up sales revenue and expenses for the year. A cash flow summary is also very helpful, but in no sense does it take the place of the other two reports. The next chapter introduces these two basic accounting reports.

2

INTRODUCING THE BALANCE SHEET AND INCOME STATEMENT

Financial Condition and Profit Reports

Managers, creditors, and investors need an accounting report that summarizes the present financial condition of the business. And they need a summary report that presents the correct sales revenue and expenses for the period just ended, to know the correct profit for the period. A cash flow statement, though very useful in its own right, does not provide the information needed concerning financial condition and profit performance.

Financial condition is presented in a report called the *Balance Sheet*. The profit performance summary is called the *Income Statement*. Both are called financial statements, or just "financials." Alternative titles for the Balance Sheet include the *Statement of Financial Condition* and the *Statement of Financial Position*. Likewise, the Income Statement may be called the *Earnings Statement* or the *Statement of Operations*. An older term, not used as often today, is the *Profit & Loss Statement*. Minor variations on all these titles are common.

Exhibit B presents the Balance Sheet and Exhibit C presents the Income Statement of the same company whose cash flows are shown in Exhibit A. The form and content of the Balance Sheet and Income Statement apply to a very broad range of manufacturers, wholesalers, and retailers. These financial statements are quite typical for any business that buys or makes products that are then sold to their customers. In others words, the two accounting reports summarize the financial condition and profit-making activity of a company that deals in products.

In addition to the Balance Sheet and Income Statement a business also reports a third financial statement—the *Cash Flow Statement*, which summarizes cash inflows and outflows for the year. The cash flows of the company in our example have already been presented in Chapter 1. The format of this third financial statement and its connections with the other two main financial statements will be explained later, after we've gone through the Balance Sheet and Income Statement.

EXHIBIT B - BALANCE SHEET AT END OF MOST RECENT YEAR OF BUSINESS

Current Assets			Current Liabilities		
Cash		$ 256,663	Accounts Payable		$ 388,834
Accounts Receivable		578,754	Accrued Expenses		188,539
Inventory		978,094	Income Tax Payable		13,394
Prepaid Expenses		117,176	Short-Term Notes Payable		425,000
Total Current Assets		$1,930,687	Total Current Liabilities		$1,015,767
			Long-Term Notes Payable		$ 550,000
Property, Plant & Equipment					
Land, Building, Machines,					
Equipment and Furniture	$1,986,450		**Stockholders' Equity**		
Accumulated Depreciation	(452,140)	$1,534,310	Capital Stock	$ 725,000	
			Retained Earnings	1,174,230	$1,899,230
Total Assets		$3,464,997	Total Liabilities & Stockholders' Equity		$3,464,997

EXHIBIT C - INCOME STATEMENT FOR MOST RECENT YEAR

Sales Revenue	$6,019,040
Cost of Goods Sold Expense	3,912,376
Gross Margin	$2,106,664
Operating Expenses	1,523,288
Operating Earnings Before Depreciation	$ 583,376
Depreciation Expense	112,792
Operating Earnings	$ 470,584
Interest Expense	76,650
Earnings Before Income Tax	$ 393,934
Income Tax Expense	133,938
Net Income	$ 259,996

Income Statement

The Income Statement summarizes sales revenue and expenses over a period of time—for one year in Exhibit C. All the dollar amounts reported in this financial statement are cumulative totals for the period. The top line is gross proceeds, or total revenue from sales to customers. The bottom line is *net income* (also called net earnings), which is the final profit remaining after *all* expenses are deducted from sales revenue.

The Income Statement is designed to be read in a step-down manner, like walking down stairs. Each step down is a deduction of one or more expenses. The first step deducts the cost of goods (products) sold from the revenue from the goods sold, which gives the line called *gross margin* (sometimes called gross profit). This measure of profit is called "gross" because several other expenses are not yet deducted.

Next, operating expenses and then depreciation expense are deducted, giving *operating earnings* before the interest and income tax expenses. Deducting interest expense from operating earnings gives *earnings before income tax*. Subtracting income tax expense from this gives the final step down to *net income*.

The Income Statement shown in Exhibit C reports five profit lines—gross margin, operating earnings before depreci-ation, operating earnings, earnings before income tax, and, finally, net income. However, some companies report only two profit lines. They add together all expenses below the gross margin line into one total amount, which is subtracted from gross margin to go directly to net income. There's no standard rule; reporting practices differ. The five-line format in Exhibit C is useful in the following discussion.

The final bottom-line profit measure in the Income Statement is simply sales revenue less all expenses. Is it true and accurate? This depends on whether sales revenue is measured correctly for the period *and* whether every expense is measured correctly for the period. These basic accounting measurement rules are discussed briefly at this point:

Sales Revenue—total amount received or to be received later from customers from the sales of products and services during the period. Sales revenue is net of (excludes) the following: discounts off list prices, prompt payment discounts, sales returns, and any other allowances or deductions from the original sales prices. Sales taxes are not included in Sales Revenue, nor are excise taxes that might apply.

Cost of Goods Sold Expense—total cost of the goods sold to customers during the period. Also, the cost of goods that were not sold but were shoplifted, stolen, or are otherwise missing, as well as write-offs and write-downs due to damage or obsolescence, are included in the Cost of Goods Sold Expense for the year. So this expense usually includes an extra charge for goods that did not produce any sales revenue during the period.

Operating Expenses—broadly speaking, every expense other than Cost of Goods Sold, Depreciation, Interest, and Income Tax. *Warning:* reporting practices for these expenses are not uniform. In Exhibit C only one total expense amount is reported for all operating expenses. But, in many cases, two or more may be reported. For example, marketing expenses may be separated from administration and general expenses, which is quite proper. Even in a relatively small business, there are hundreds of different operating expenses, some rather large and some very small. They range from salaries and wages of employees (large) to legal fees (preferably, small).

Depreciation Expense—fraction of the original cost of long-term operating assets (buildings, machinery, equipment, tools, furniture, and fixtures) that is recorded to expense during this period; this is the "charge" for using the assets during the period.

Interest Expense—total amount of interest on debt (interest-bearing liabilities) for the period. Other types of financing charges may also be included, such as loan-fees.

Income Tax Expense—total amount due the government on the taxable income earned by the business during the period. This is determined by multiplying the taxable income for the period by the appropriate tax rates, less any credits (direct deductions). Income Tax Expense does not include other types of taxes, such as unemployment and social security taxes on payroll and property taxes, which are included in Operating Expenses. However, state income taxes are included.

Balance Sheet

The Balance Sheet format in Exhibit B follows fairly standardized and uniform rules of classification and ordering. (The Income Statement is somewhat more flexible.) Financial institutions, public utilities, railroads, and a few other rather specialized businesses use different Balance Sheet formats. But the large majority of industrial and retail businesses follow the Balance Sheet format shown in Exhibit B.

On the left side the Balance Sheet lists assets. On the right side it lists liabilities and owners' equity. The owners of a corporation are its stockholders. So, owners' equity is called stockholders' equity. Each separate asset, liability, and owners' equity reported in the Balance Sheet is called an *account*. Every account has a name (title) and a dollar amount, which is called its balance. For instance, from Exhibit B:

Name of Account	*Amount (Balance) of Account*
Inventory	$978,094

The other dollar amounts in the Balance Sheet are not accounts; they are subtotals or totals from adding (or subtracting) balances of accounts. A line is drawn to indicate that a subtotal or total is being taken.

The Balance Sheet is prepared at the close of business on the last day of the Income Statement period. If, for example, the Income Statement is for the year ending June 30, 1994, the Balance Sheet is prepared at midnight June 30, 1994. The accounts' balances reported in the Balance Sheet are the amounts at that precise moment in time. The financial situation of the business is "frozen" for one split second, as it were.

The Balance Sheet does not report the total flows into and out of the assets, liabilities, and owners' equity accounts during the period. Only the ending balance at the Balance Sheet date is reported for each account. For example, the company has an ending Cash balance of $256,663 (see Exhibit B). Can you tell the cash receipts and disbursements during the year? No, not from the Balance Sheet.

Balance Sheet accounts are subdivided into the following classes, or basic groups, in the following order of presentation:

Left Side	*Right Side*
(1) Current Assets	(1) Current Liabilities
(2) Property, Plant & Equipment	(2) Long-term Liabilities
(3) Other Assets	(3) Stockholders' Equity

Current Assets are cash and those other assets that will be converted into cash during one operating cycle. Assets not directly involved in the operating cycle (such as marketable securities or receivables from employees) are included in Current Assets if they will be converted into cash during the coming year.

The operating cycle refers to the sequence of acquiring products, holding the products until sale, selling the products, waiting to collect the receivables from the sales and, finally, receiving the cash from the customers. This sequence is the most basic process of a business' operations; it's repeated over and over. The operating cycle may be short, only 60 days or less, or it may be relatively long, perhaps 180 days or more.

Although not as common today, in the past the assets grouped in the category Property, Plant & Equipment were called *Fixed Assets*. However, this term is not satisfactory. Fixed assets are not really fixed or permanent, excepting the land owned by a business. More accurately, these are long-term operating assets used by a business over several years, such as buildings, machinery and equipment, trucks, forklifts, office furniture, computers, and so on.

The cost of a long-lived operating asset, excepting land, is gradually charged off over its useful life. The cumulative amount of its cost that has been charged off since the date of acquisition up to the Balance Sheet date is in the Accumulated Depreciation account. The balance in this account is deducted from the original cost balance in the asset account.

Other Assets is a catchall class for those assets that don't fit in either the Current Assets or Property, Plant & Equipment. The company in this example does not have any other assets.

The official definition of *Current Liabilities* runs 200 words, plus a long footnote. Briefly, these are short-term debts that for the most part depend on the conversion of current assets into cash for their payment. Also, other debts that will come due within one year from the Balance Sheet date are put in the Current Liabilities class. There are four accounts in this class—see Exhibit B again.

Long-Term Liabilities are debts whose maturity dates are more than one year after the Balance Sheet date. There's only one account in this class (see Exhibit B again). Either in the Balance Sheet or in a footnote to the statement, the maturity dates and other relevant provisions of all long-term liabilities should be disclosed. To simplify, no footnotes are presented here. Footnotes are discussed in Chapter 17.

Liabilities are claims on the assets of a business; cash or other assets that will be converted into cash later will be used to pay the liabilities. It's apparent, therefore, that liabilities should be accounted for in the Balance Sheet.

Liabilities are also *sources* of assets. Clearly, the total assets of a company increase when it borrows money. Also, a business has liabilities for unpaid expenses. The company has not had to use some of its assets to pay these liabilities.

The other reason for reporting liabilities in the Balance Sheet is to account for the sources of the company's assets—to answer the question: Where did the company's total assets come from? A complete Balance Sheet accounting requires that all sources of the company's assets be accounted for.

In addition to liabilities, the other basic source of a company's total assets is from its owners. The *Stockholders' Equity* class reveals the rest of the sources of a company's total assets.

There are two basic stockholders' equity accounts—Capital Stock and Retained Earnings.

When the owners (the stockholders in the case of a corporation) invest capital in the business, the Capital Stock account is increased.* The amount of net income (profit) earned by a business less the amount distributed to its owners from the profit gives the amount of earnings retained in the business. This amount is recorded in the Retained Earnings account. The nature of Retained Earnings is confusing and, therefore, is explained very carefully later in the book at the appropriate places.

*Many corporations issue par value stock shares; when they issue stock shares for more than par value the excess may be reported in a second stock account called Additional Paid-In Capital, or Paid-In Capital in Excess of Par Value. This is not shown in the example. This separation between the two accounts has little practical significance.

3

PROFIT
ISN'T EVERYTHING

The Threefold Task of Managers:
Profit, Financial Condition, and Cash Flow

The Income Statement reports the profit performance of the business. The ability of managers to make sales and to control expenses, and thereby to earn profit, is measured in the Income Statement. Clearly, earning an adequate profit is the key for survival and the manager's most important imperative. But the bottom line is not the end of the manager's task.

Managers must also control the *financial condition* of the business. This means keeping the assets and liabilities within proper limits and proportions relative to each other and relative to the sales and expense levels of the company. And, managers must *prevent cash shortages* that would cause the business to default on its liabilities or to miss its payroll.

The business manager really has a *threefold task:* earning profit, controlling the company's financial condition, and preventing "cashouts." Profit performance alone does not guarantee survival. In other words, you can't manage profit without also managing the changes in financial condition caused by the sales and expenses that produce your profit. Furthermore, the profit-making activity may actually put a temporary drain on cash rather than provide cash inflow.

The business manager should use the Income Statement to evaluate profit performance and to ask a whole raft of profit-oriented questions. Did sales revenue meet the goals and objectives for the period? Why did sales revenue increase compared to last period? Which expenses increased more or less than they should have? And so on. These profit management questions are absolutely essential. But the manager can't stop at the end of these questions.

Beyond the profit analysis, the business manager has to move on to *financial condition* analysis and *cash flow* analysis. In large business organizations, responsibility for financial condition and cash flow usually is separated from profit responsibility. The chief financial officer (CFO) is responsible for financial condition and cash flow; other organization units are responsible for sales and costs. In these large companies the chief executive and the board of directors must oversee and approve the decisions of the CFO. But most of the details can be and usually are delegated to the CFO.

In middle-size and smaller businesses, however, the top-level manager or the owner/manager is directly and totally responsible for financial condition and cash flow. There's no one else to delegate these responsibilities to.

The Trouble with
Conventional Financial Statements

Unfortunately, the typical financial statements prepared by accountants do not "pave the way" for financial condition and cash flow analyses. Conventional financial statements are not ready-made for these purposes.

The Balance Sheet and Income Statement for a business, such as shown in Exhibits B and C, do not leave a clear trail of the "cross-over effects" between these two basic financial statements. The statements are presented on the assumption that the reader understands these couplings and linkages between the two statements and that the reader will make the appropriate connections and comparisons.

The Balance Sheet and Income Statement need to be accompanied by a cash flow statement. Only recently (1987) did the rule-making body of the accounting profession make the cash flow statement one of the *required* statements in financial reports. In the opinion of many, this change was long overdue. Managers, as well as creditors and investors, clearly need a cash flow statement that summarizes the major sources and uses of cash during the period.

Chapter 1 has already explained that cash flows are the natural center of gravity for business managers. Exhibit A (page 3) shows the cash flow summary for the company. To be most useful, however, the cash flow summary needs to be tied in with the company's Balance Sheet and Income Statement to understand the interlocking of all three statements.

EXHIBIT D - MASTER EXHIBIT

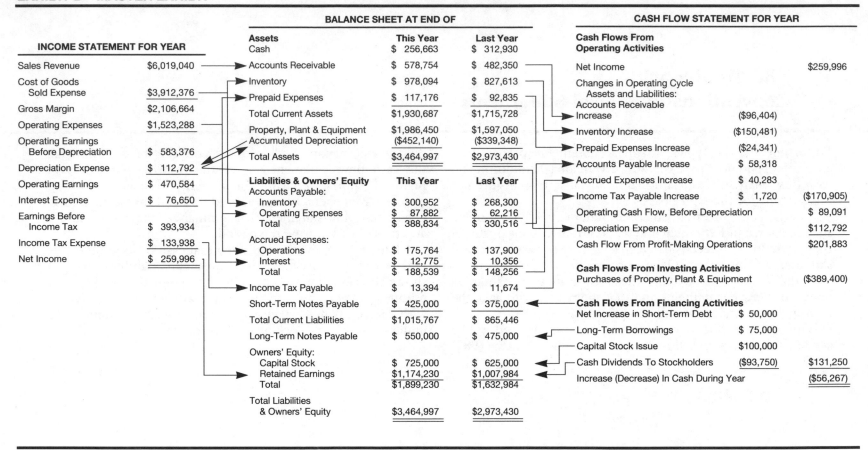

BALANCE SHEET AT END OF

CASH FLOW STATEMENT FOR YEAR

INCOME STATEMENT FOR YEAR

Sales Revenue	$6,019,040
Cost of Goods Sold Expense	$3,912,376
Gross Margin	$2,106,664
Operating Expenses	$1,523,288
Operating Earnings Before Depreciation	$ 583,376
Depreciation Expense	$ 112,792
Operating Earnings	$ 470,584
Interest Expense	$ 76,650
Earnings Before Income Tax	$ 393,934
Income Tax Expense	$ 133,938
Net Income	$ 259,996

Balance Sheet

Assets	This Year	Last Year
Cash	$ 256,663	$ 312,930
Accounts Receivable	$ 578,754	$ 482,350
Inventory	$ 978,094	$ 827,613
Prepaid Expenses	$ 117,176	$ 92,835
Total Current Assets	$1,930,687	$1,715,728
Property, Plant & Equipment	$1,986,450	$1,597,050
Accumulated Depreciation	($452,140)	($339,348)
Total Assets	$3,464,997	$2,973,430

Liabilities & Owners' Equity	This Year	Last Year
Accounts Payable:		
Inventory	$ 300,952	$ 268,300
Operating Expenses	$ 87,882	$ 62,216
Total	$ 388,834	$ 330,516
Accrued Expenses:		
Operations	$ 175,764	$ 137,900
Interest	$ 12,775	$ 10,356
Total	$ 188,539	$ 148,256
Income Tax Payable	$ 13,394	$ 11,674
Short-Term Notes Payable	$ 425,000	$ 375,000
Total Current Liabilities	$1,015,767	$ 865,446
Long-Term Notes Payable	$ 550,000	$ 475,000
Owners' Equity:		
Capital Stock	$ 725,000	$ 625,000
Retained Earnings	$1,174,230	$1,007,984
Total	$1,899,230	$1,632,984
Total Liabilities & Owners' Equity	$3,464,997	$2,973,430

Cash Flows From Operating Activities

Net Income		$259,996
Changes in Operating Cycle Assets and Liabilities:		
Accounts Receivable Increase	($96,404)	
Inventory Increase	($150,481)	
Prepaid Expenses Increase	($24,341)	
Accounts Payable Increase	$ 58,318	
Accrued Expenses Increase	$ 40,283	
Income Tax Payable Increase	$ 1,720	($170,905)
Operating Cash Flow, Before Depreciation		$ 89,091
Depreciation Expense		$112,792
Cash Flow From Profit-Making Operations		$201,883

Cash Flows From Investing Activities

Purchases of Property, Plant & Equipment		($389,400)

Cash Flows From Financing Activities

Net Increase in Short-Term Debt	$ 50,000	
Long-Term Borrowings	$ 75,000	
Capital Stock Issue	$100,000	
Cash Dividends To Stockholders	($93,750)	$131,250
Increase (Decrease) In Cash During Year		($56,267)

A New Layout to Learn the Interlocking
Nature of the Three Basic Financial Statements

Please look at Exhibit D on page 18. These are the same financial statements shown earlier, although they have been rearranged into a new layout. Also, the Balance Sheet at the end of last year is presented for comparison.

Lines of connection between the three statements are drawn in; these serve as "tether lines" in the following discussion. To help show these lines more clearly, the Balance Sheet is positioned in the middle and it is shown in the vertical (or, "report form") format—assets are on the top, and liabilities and stockholders' equity are on the bottom. The Income Statement is placed on the left and the Cash Flow Statement on the right.

Notice that the format of the Cash Flow Statement is changed quite a bit from that first introduced in Chapter 1. Basically, the Cash Flow Statement now uses the bottom-line net income from the Income Statement as the starting point. This net income figure is then "adjusted" to arrive at the cash flow from the profit-making operations of the company for the year.

In Exhibit D, Accounts Payable and Accrued Expenses are divided into two parts each to show the two separate sources of each (which are explained in later chapters). A few tether lines are not drawn in (they will be made clear in later chapters), to avoid crossing over too many other lines.

So now we have all three financial statements tied together, and the important relationships among the three are made clear.

Financial statements are *not* reported to managers or to creditors and investors in the manner shown in Exhibit D. Accountants assume that interested readers mentally fill in the lines of connection and make the comparisons shown in Exhibit D. Accountants probably assume too much. It takes a fair amount of understanding and some experience to know which relationships are important to look for and what these comparisons mean.

Until managers and other users develop such skills in reading financial statements, the "octopus" format shown in Exhibit D, which shows the "tentacles" of connection, is very useful. The format certainly is helpful in explaining financial statements.

The Exhibit is repeated at the beginning of the following chapters, each of which focuses on one basic line of connection. For example, Chapter 4 explores the very important linkage between Sales Revenue in the Income Statement and Accounts Receivable in the Balance Sheet.

Exhibit D looks rather formidable at first glance, doesn't it? Like most reports with a lot of detail, you have to take it one piece at a time, rather than in one quick sweep. It's like looking at a chess board in the middle of a game. You have to study each piece in relation to the other relevant pieces before you can see the overall pattern and situation. We'll go carefully through each step, one at a time, in the following chapters.

EXHIBIT D - MASTER EXHIBIT

INCOME STATEMENT FOR YEAR

Sales Revenue	$6,019,040
Cost of Goods Sold Expense	$3,912,376
Gross Margin	$2,106,664
Operating Expenses	$1,523,288
Operating Earnings Before Depreciation	$ 583,376
Depreciation Expense	$ 112,792
Operating Earnings	$ 470,584
Interest Expense	$ 76,650
Earnings Before Income Tax	$ 393,934
Income Tax Expense	$ 133,938
Net Income	$ 259,996

BALANCE SHEET AT END OF

Assets	This Year	Last Year
Cash	$ 256,663	$ 312,930
Accounts Receivable	$ 578,754	$ 482,350
Inventory	$ 978,094	$ 827,613
Prepaid Expenses	$ 117,176	$ 92,835
Total Current Assets	$1,930,687	$1,715,728
Property, Plant & Equipment	$1,986,450	$1,597,050
Accumulated Depreciation	($452,140)	($339,348)
Total Assets	$3,464,997	$2,973,430

Liabilities & Owners' Equity	This Year	Last Year
Accounts Payable:		
Inventory	$ 300,952	$ 268,300
Operating Expenses	$ 87,882	$ 62,216
Total	$ 388,834	$ 330,516
Accrued Expenses:		
Operations	$ 175,764	$ 137,900
Interest	$ 12,775	$ 10,356
Total	$ 188,539	$ 148,256
Income Tax Payable	$ 13,394	$ 11,674
Short-Term Notes Payable	$ 425,000	$ 375,000
Total Current Liabilities	$1,015,767	$ 865,446
Long-Term Notes Payable	$ 550,000	$ 475,000
Owners' Equity:		
Capital Stock	$ 725,000	$ 625,000
Retained Earnings	$1,174,230	$1,007,984
Total	$1,899,230	$1,632,984
Total Liabilities & Owners' Equity	$3,464,997	$2,973,430

CASH FLOW STATEMENT FOR YEAR

Cash Flows From Operating Activities		
Net Income		$259,996
Changes in Operating Cycle Assets and Liabilities:		
Accounts Receivable Increase	($96,404)	
Inventory Increase	($150,481)	
Prepaid Expenses Increase	($24,341)	
Accounts Payable Increase	$ 58,318	
Accrued Expenses Increase	$ 40,283	
Income Tax Payable Increase	$ 1,720	($170,905)
Operating Cash Flow, Before Depreciation		$ 89,091
Depreciation Expense		$112,792
Cash Flow From Profit-Making Operations		$201,883
Cash Flows From Investing Activities		
Purchases of Property, Plant & Equipment		($389,400)
Cash Flows From Financing Activities		
Net Increase in Short-Term Debt	$ 50,000	
Long-Term Borrowings	$ 75,000	
Capital Stock Issue	$100,000	
Cash Dividends To Stockholders	($93,750)	$131,250
Increase (Decrease) In Cash During Year		($56,267)

4

SALES REVENUE
↓
ACCOUNTS RECEIVABLE

Refer to Exhibit D—Chapter 4. This Exhibit, introduced in the preceding chapter, is presented here again for convenient reference. Because the Exhibit will be repeated in the following chapters also, the chapter number for which the Exhibit is being used is given.

Notice the two accounts connected in the Exhibit—Sales Revenue in the Income Statement and Accounts Receivable in the Balance Sheet. The relationship between the two and the nature of each are the main topics of this chapter. You'll notice that only this one line of connection is shown in the Exhibit, whereas all lines of connection are shown in the "master" Exhibit D on page 18.

In this example the company made total sales of $6,019,040 during the year. When a sale is made, the amount of the sale, which basically is sales price times the quantity sold, is recorded in Sales Revenue. This account accumulates all sales made during the year. At year-end, therefore, the balance in the account is the sum of all sales for the entire year.

Assume in this example that the company makes all its sales on credit. This means that cash is not received until sometime after the date of sale. The amount owed to the company, however, is immediately recorded in Accounts Receivable when each sale is made. The balance in this asset account is the amount of uncollected sales revenue.

Extending credit to customers creates a cash inflow lag. The balance of Accounts Receivable is the amount of this lag. Later, when cash is collected from customers, the Cash account is increased and Accounts Receivable is decreased.

By the end of the year most of the sales made during the year had been collected; the receivables had been converted into cash. Also, the Accounts Receivable at the start of the year from sales made last year were collected. But at year-end many sales had not yet been collected. The amount of these uncollected sales is the balance of Accounts Receivable at the end of the year.

Some of its customers pay quickly, to take advantage of prompt payment discounts offered by the company. (These discounts reduce its sales prices but speed up its cash receipts.) On the other hand, the typical customer waits about 5 weeks to pay the company and forgoes the prompt payment discount. The really slow customers wait 10 weeks or more to pay the company.

In sum, the company has a mixture of quick, regular, and slow-paying customers: we'll assume that the average sales credit period of this company is 5 weeks. Thus, 5 weeks of the company's sales for the year are still uncollected at year-end. So the ending balance of its Accounts Receivables is computed as follows in this example:

$$\frac{5}{52} \times \frac{\$6,019,040}{\text{Sales Revenue for year}} = \frac{\$578,754}{\text{Accounts Receivable}}$$

You'll notice in Exhibit D that the ending balance of Accounts Receivable is indeed $578,754.

The main point here is that the average sales credit period determines the size of Accounts Receivable relative to annual sales revenue. The longer the average sales credit period, the larger the Accounts Receivable.

Let's approach this key point from another direction. Using information in the financial statements, we can determine the average sales credit period. The first step is to compute the following ratio:

$$\frac{\$6,019,040 \text{ Sales Revenue for year}}{\$578,754 \text{ Accounts Receivable}} = 10.4$$

This computation gives the *Accounts Receivable turnover ratio*. This number divided into 52 weeks gives the average sales credit period expressed in number of weeks:

$$\frac{52 \text{ weeks}}{10.4 \text{ Accounts Receivable turnover ratio}} = 5 \text{ weeks}$$

Time is the essence of the matter here. What interests the manager, and the company's creditors and investors as well, is how long it takes on average to turn its receivables into cash. The Accounts Receivable turnover ratio is most meaningful when it is used to determine the number of weeks (or days) it takes the company to convert its receivables into cash.

You may argue that 5 weeks is too long an average sales credit period for the company. This is precisely the point: What should it be? The manager in charge has to decide whether the average sales credit period is getting out of hand. The manager can shorten credit terms, shut off credit to slow payers, or step up collection efforts.

This is not the place to discuss customer credit policies relative to selling strategies and customer relations, which would take us far into the fields of marketing and credits and collections. But to make an important point here: Assume that without losing any sales the company's average sales credit period

had been only 4 weeks, instead of the 5 weeks assumed in the financial statements of the company. In this case the ending balance of Accounts Receivable would have been $115,751 less, which is the average sales revenue per week ($6,019,040 ÷ 52 weeks = $115,751). The company would have collected $115,751 more cash during the year.

With such additional cash inflow the company could have borrowed $115,751 less. At a 10% annual interest rate this would have saved $11,575 interest expense before income tax. Or the owners could have invested $115,751 less in the business and put their money elsewhere. The point is, of course, that capital has a high cost. Excess Accounts Receivable means that excess debt, or excess owners' equity capital, is being used by the business.

A slow-up in collecting customers' receivables, or a deliberate shift in company policy allowing longer credit terms, would cause Accounts Receivable to increase. Additional capital would have to be secured, or the company would have to try to get by on a smaller cash balance.

If you were the manager in this example you would have to decide whether the size of Accounts Receivable, being 5 weeks of annual sales revenue, is consistent with the company's sales credit terms and collection policies. Perhaps 5 weeks is too long and you need to take action. If you were a creditor or an investor, you should be very interested in whether the manager is allowing the average sales credit period to get out of control. And you should be interested in any major change in the average sales credit period that may signal a major change in the company's policies.

INCOME STATEMENT FOR YEAR

Sales Revenue	$6,019,040
Cost of Goods Sold Expense	$3,912,376
Gross Margin	$2,106,664
Operating Expenses	$1,523,288
Operating Earnings Before Depreciation	$ 583,376
Depreciation Expense	$ 112,792
Operating Earnings	$ 470,584
Interest Expense	$ 76,650
Earnings Before Income Tax	$ 393,934
Income Tax Expense	$ 133,938
Net Income	$ 259,996

BALANCE SHEET AT END OF

Assets	This Year	Last Year
Cash	$ 256,663	$ 312,930
Accounts Receivable	$ 578,754	$ 482,350
Inventory	$ 978,094	$ 827,613
Prepaid Expenses	$ 117,176	$ 92,835
Total Current Assets	$1,930,687	$1,715,728
Property, Plant & Equipment	$1,986,450	$1,597,050
Accumulated Depreciation	($452,140)	($339,348)
Total Assets	$3,464,997	$2,973,430

Liabilities & Owners' Equity	This Year	Last Year
Accounts Payable:		
Inventory	$ 300,952	$ 268,300
Operating Expenses	$ 87,882	$ 62,216
Total	$ 388,834	$ 330,516
Accrued Expenses:		
Operations	$ 175,764	$ 137,900
Interest	$ 12,775	$ 10,356
Total	$ 188,539	$ 148,256
Income Tax Payable	$ 13,394	$ 11,674
Short-Term Notes Payable	$ 425,000	$ 375,000
Total Current Liabilities	$1,015,767	$ 865,446
Long-Term Notes Payable	$ 550,000	$ 475,000
Owners' Equity:		
Capital Stock	$ 725,000	$ 625,000
Retained Earnings	$1,174,230	$1,007,984
Total	$1,899,230	$1,632,984
Total Liabilities & Owners' Equity	$3,464,997	$2,973,430

CASH FLOW STATEMENT FOR YEAR

Cash Flows From Operating Activities		
Net Income		$259,996
Changes in Operating Cycle Assets and Liabilities:		
Accounts Receivable Increase	($96,404)	
Inventory Increase	($150,481)	
Prepaid Expenses Increase	($24,341)	
Accounts Payable Increase	$ 58,318	
Accrued Expenses Increase	$ 40,283	
Income Tax Payable Increase	$ 1,720	($170,905)
Operating Cash Flow, Before Depreciation		$ 89,091
Depreciation Expense		$112,792
Cash Flow From Profit-Making Operations		$201,883
Cash Flows From Investing Activities		
Purchases of Property, Plant & Equipment		($389,400)
Cash Flows From Financing Activities		
Net Increase in Short-Term Debt	$ 50,000	
Long-Term Borrowings	$ 75,000	
Capital Stock Issue	$100,000	
Cash Dividends To Stockholders	($93,750)	$131,250
Increase (Decrease) In Cash During Year		($56,267)

5

COST OF GOODS SOLD EXPENSE

INVENTORY

To begin, refer to Exhibit D—Chapter 5. Notice the two accounts connected—Cost of Goods Sold Expense in the Income Statement and Inventory in the Balance Sheet. The relationship between these two accounts and the nature of each are the topics of this chapter.

Cost of Goods Sold Expense is, by far, the largest expense in the Income Statement. It's deducted from Sales Revenue to determine *gross margin*, which is the first of the five profit lines reported in the Income Statement.

Gross margin is called gross because no other expenses have been deducted. Only the cost of buying (or making) the product is deducted from sales revenue at this point. Gross margin is the starting point for earning an adequate final profit (net income). In other words, the first step is to sell the products (goods) for enough gross margin so that all the other expenses of the business can be covered. These other expenses are discussed in later chapters.

In this example the company earned a gross margin equal to 35% of its sales revenue:

$$\frac{\$2,106,664 \text{ Gross Margin}}{\$6,019,040 \text{ Sales Revenue}} = 35\%$$

The company sells a mix of different products, not all at the same gross profit margin (percent of sales price). In total, for all products sold during the year, its average gross profit is 35%, which is fairly typical for a broad cross section of businesses.

To sell products a business must carry a stock of products, on hand and ready for delivery to its customers. This stock of products, the goods being held for sale, is called *Inventory*. So

making sales causes Inventory to appear in the Balance Sheet. The line of connection is not with Sales Revenue, but rather with Cost of Goods Sold Expense, because Inventory is reported at cost in the Balance Sheet, *not* at its sales value.

When a company buys products, its Inventory account is increased by the cost of the goods. This cost is kept in the Inventory asset account until the items are sold and delivered to customers when making sales. At this time the cost is removed from the asset and charged to Cost of Goods Sold Expense. (If products become definitely unsalable or are stolen, their cost is removed from Inventory and charged to expense.)

The Inventory balance at year-end—$978,094 in this example, as shown in Exhibit D—is the cost of products awaiting sale next year. The $3,912,376 deducted from Sales Revenue in the Income Statement is the cost of the goods that were sold during the year; of course, none of these products are on hand in Inventory at year-end.

Some of the company's products may come in and go out in a week or two; other goods may stay in stock 4 months or longer. As usual, holding periods differ for different products. The company's average inventory holding period, given the mix of all its products, is assumed to be 13 weeks in this example.

In other words, the quantity of goods in inventory is enough for 13 weeks of average sales. As just mentioned, inventory is recorded at cost. So 13 weeks of sales here means 13 weeks of cost of goods sold, not 13 weeks of sales revenue. Knowing that the average inventory holding period is 13 weeks, the company's Inventory balance is computed as follows in this example:

$$\frac{13}{52} \times \frac{\$3,912,376}{\text{Cost of Goods Sold for year}} = \frac{\$978,094}{\text{Inventory}}$$

You'll notice in Exhibit D—Chapter 5 that the ending balance of Inventory is indeed $978,094.

The main point is that the average inventory holding period determines the size of Inventory relative to annual cost of goods sold. The longer the holding period, the larger the Inventory.

Let's approach this key point from another direction. Using information available from the financial statements, we can determine the average inventory holding period. The first step is to compute the following ratio:

$$\frac{\$3,912,376 \text{ Cost of Goods Sold Expense for year}}{\$978,094 \text{ Inventory}} = 4.00$$

This gives the *Inventory turnover ratio*. This number divided into 52 weeks gives the average inventory holding period expressed in number of weeks:

$$\frac{52 \text{ weeks}}{4.00 \text{ Inventory turnover ratio}} = 13 \text{ weeks}$$

Time is the essence of the matter here, as it is with the average sales credit period discussed in the preceding chapter. What interests the manager, and the company's creditors and investors as well, is how long the company holds an average item of inventory before it's sold. The Inventory turnover ratio is most meaningful when it is used to determine the number of weeks (or days) it takes the company before the inventory is sold.

Is 13 weeks too long? Should the company's average inventory holding period be shorter? This is precisely the key question that business managers, creditors, and investors should be concerned with. If the holding period is longer than really necessary, too much capital is being tied up in inventory and, as already mentioned, capital has a high cost. Or the company may be cash poor because it has too much money in inventory and not enough in the bank.

If the company could reduce its inventory holding period to, say, 10 weeks, $225,714 capital would be saved ($75,238 Cost of Goods Sold Expense per week × 3 weeks less Inventory = $225,714 less capital required). However, with only 10 weeks average inventory, the company may be unable to make many sales because certain products were not available when needed. In other words, if the average inventory holding period is too low, the result may be *stock-outs* of certain goods, or not being able to get the goods as soon as needed to make sales. The cost of carrying inventory has to be balanced against the profit opportunities lost by not having the products in stock ready for sale.

In short, managers, and creditors and investors as well, should be concerned that the average inventory holding period is neither too high nor too low. If too high, capital is being wasted; if too low, profit opportunities are being missed. Comparisons with other companies in the same line of business and historical trends provide the guidelines for testing a company's inventory holding period.

EXHIBIT D—CHAPTER 6

INCOME STATEMENT FOR YEAR	
Sales Revenue	$6,019,040
Cost of Goods Sold Expense	$3,912,376
Gross Margin	$2,106,664
Operating Expenses	$1,523,288
Operating Earnings Before Depreciation	$ 583,376
Depreciation Expense	$ 112,792
Operating Earnings	$ 470,584
Interest Expense	$ 76,650
Earnings Before Income Tax	$ 393,934
Income Tax Expense	$ 133,938
Net Income	$ 259,996

BALANCE SHEET AT END OF

Assets	This Year	Last Year
Cash	$ 256,663	$ 312,930
Accounts Receivable	$ 578,754	$ 482,350
Inventory	$ 978,094	$ 827,613
Prepaid Expenses	$ 117,176	$ 92,835
Total Current Assets	$1,930,687	$1,715,728
Property Plant, & Equipment	$1,986,450	$1,597,050
Accumulated Depreciation	($452,140)	($339,348)
Total Assets	$3,464,997	$2,973,430

Liabilities & Owners' Equity	This Year	Last Year
Accounts Payable:		
Inventory	$ 300,952	$ 268,300
Operating Expenses	$ 87,882	$ 62,216
Total	$ 388,834	$ 330,516
Accrued Expenses:		
Operations	$ 175,764	$ 137,900
Interest	$ 12,775	$ 10,356
Total	$ 188,539	$ 148,256
Income Tax Payable	$ 13,394	$ 11,674
Short-Term Notes Payable	$ 425,000	$ 375,000
Total Current Liabilities	$1,015,767	$ 865,446
Long-Term Notes Payable	$ 550,000	$ 475,000
Owners' Equity:		
Capital Stock	$ 725,000	$ 625,000
Retained Earnings	$1,174,230	$1,007,984
Total	$1,899,230	$1,632,984
Total Liabilities & Owners' Equity	$3,464,997	$2,973,430

CASH FLOW STATEMENT FOR YEAR

Cash Flows From Operating Activities		
Net Income		$259,996
Changes in Operating Cycle Assets and Liabilities:		
Accounts Receivable Increase	($96,404)	
Inventory Increase	($150,481)	
Prepaid Expenses Increase	($24,341)	
Accounts Payable Increase	$ 58,318	
Accrued Expenses Increase	$ 40,283	
Income Tax Payable Increase	$ 1,720	($170,905)
Operating Cash Flow, Before Depreciation		$ 89,091
Depreciation Expense		$112,792
Cash Flow From Profit-Making Operations		$201,883
Cash Flows From Investing Activities		
Purchases of Property, Plant & Equipment		($389,400)
Cash Flows From Financing Activities		
Net Increase in Short-Term Debt	$ 50,000	
Long-Term Borrowings	$ 75,000	
Capital Stock Issue	$100,000	
Cash Dividends To Stockholders	($93,750)	$131,250
Increase (Decrease) In Cash During Year		($56,267)

6

INVENTORY
↓
ACCOUNTS PAYABLE

Please note in Exhibit D—Chapter 6 the line linking Inventory with Accounts Payable in the Balance Sheet, including the broken line from Cost of Goods Sold Expense.

To set the stage here, let's review very briefly the last two chapters. The sales prices of goods (products) sold are accumulated in the Sales Revenue account. Sales made on credit cause Accounts Receivable; the longer the credit period, the larger the Accounts Receivable. The cost of goods sold is accumulated in the Cost of Goods Sold Expense account. Products must be bought and held in Inventory before they are sold. The longer the holding period, the larger the Inventory.

Inventory is closely related to Cost of Goods Sold Expense; it's also closely related to Accounts Payable. This second relationship is the main topic of this chapter.

Businesses purchase their inventory on credit. COD (cash on delivery) purchase terms are not often encountered, unless a company is in financial trouble or has a lousy credit rating. So the typical business does not make immediate payment for its inventory purchases. (Manufacturers buy their raw materials and production supplies on credit; the main points in the following discussion apply to these types of items as well.)

When inventory is purchased on credit, the liability for the amount of goods bought is recorded in *Accounts Payable*. As mentioned in the preceding chapter, the cost is also recorded in Inventory; both the asset and the liability increase the same amount.

Some purchases are paid quickly, to take advantage of prompt payment discounts offered by suppliers. But many bills are not paid until 2 months or so after purchase. Based on its payments experience and policies, a business can determine the average credit period it waits before paying for its inventory purchases. In this example, we'll assume that the average inventory purchases credit period is 4 weeks.

In other words, from the date of purchase to the date of payment is 4 weeks on average. So the last 4 weeks of inventory purchases had not been paid yet at year-end. Purchases may vary week to week; in this example, however, we assume purchases are fairly equal week to week to replace goods sold and keep inventory at a stable level.

The average cost of goods sold per week (equal to purchases per week here) is $75,238 ($3,912,376 cost of goods sold per year ÷ 52 weeks = $75,238). So the Accounts Payable amount from inventory purchases is computed as follows in this example:

$75,238	×	4 weeks	= $300,952
Cost of Goods Sold (and purchases) per week		inventory purchase credit period	Accounts Payable

See this connection in Exhibit D—Chapter 6.

Sometimes at year-end the amount of Accounts Payable from inventory purchases may be higher than normal. The company may have made a large purchase just before year-end because of a supply shortage forecast or in anticipation of price increases. Or, the company may have deliberately slowed down payment of its bills toward year-end to conserve its cash balance, which would cause a temporary bulge in Accounts Payable.

INCOME STATEMENT FOR YEAR

Sales Revenue	$6,019,040
Cost of Goods Sold Expense	$3,912,376
Gross Margin	$2,106,664
Operating Expenses	$1,523,288
Operating Earnings Before Depreciation	$ 583,376
Depreciation Expense	$ 112,792
Operating Earnings	$ 470,584
Interest Expense	$ 76,650
Earnings Before Income Tax	$ 393,934
Income Tax Expense	$ 133,938
Net Income	$ 259,996

BALANCE SHEET AT END OF

Assets	This Year	Last Year
Cash	$ 256,663	$ 312,930
Accounts Receivable	$ 578,754	$ 482,350
Inventory	$ 978,094	$ 827,613
Prepaid Expenses	$ 117,176	$ 92,835
Total Current Assets	$1,930,687	$1,715,728
Property, Plant & Equipment	$1,986,450	$1,597,050
Accumulated Depreciation	($452,140)	($339,348)
Total Assets	$3,464,997	$2,973,430

Liabilities & Owners' Equity	This Year	Last Year
Accounts Payable:		
Inventory	$ 300,952	$ 268,300
Operating Expenses	$ 87,882	$ 62,216
Total	$ 388,834	$ 330,516
Accrued Expenses:		
Operations	$ 175,764	$ 137,900
Interest	$ 12,775	$ 10,356
Total	$ 188,539	$ 148,256
Income Tax Payable	$ 13,394	$ 11,674
Short-Term Notes Payable	$ 425,000	$ 375,000
Total Current Liabilities	$1,015,767	$ 865,446
Long-Term Notes Payable	$ 550,000	$ 475,000
Owners' Equity:		
Capital Stock	$ 725,000	$ 625,000
Retained Earnings	$1,174,230	$1,007,984
Total	$1,899,230	$1,632,984
Total Liabilities & Owners' Equity	$3,464,997	$2,973,430

CASH FLOW STATEMENT FOR YEAR

Cash Flows From Operating Activities

Net Income		$259,996
Changes in Operating Cycle Assets and Liabilities:		
Accounts Receivable Increase	($96,404)	
Inventory Increase	($150,481)	
Prepaid Expenses Increase	($24,341)	
Accounts Payable Increase	$ 58,318	
Accrued Expenses Increase	$ 40,283	
Income Tax Payable Increase	$ 1,720	($170,905)
Operating Cash Flow, Before Depreciation		$ 89,091
Depreciation Expense		$112,792
Cash Flow From Profit-Making Operations		$201,883

Cash Flows From Investing Activities

Purchases of Property, Plant & Equipment		($389,400)

Cash Flows From Financing Activities

Net Increase in Short-Term Debt	$ 50,000	
Long-Term Borrowings	$ 75,000	
Capital Stock Issue	$100,000	
Cash Dividends To Stockholders	($93,750)	$131,250
Increase (Decrease) In Cash During Year		($56,267)

7

OPERATING EXPENSES
↓
ACCOUNTS PAYABLE

Have you looked at Exhibit D—Chapter 7? Note the linkage between Operating Expenses in the Income Statement and Accounts Payable in the Balance Sheet. This relationship and the nature of these two accounts are discussed in this chapter.

Operating Expenses is a conglomerate account in the Income Statement, which includes all the different expenses of running the business *except* Depreciation Expense. The Depreciation Expense is unique and is reported separately from the Operating Expenses. Depreciation is discussed in Chapter 10.

Included under the umbrella of Operating Expenses are the following (in no particular order):

♦ Rent of land and buildings

♦ Wages and salaries paid officers, office employees, salespersons, warehouse workers, and so on

♦ Payroll taxes and other fringe benefit costs of labor

♦ Office and data processing supplies and machine rentals

♦ Property taxes

♦ Telephone

♦ Utilities (water, gas, electricity)

♦ General liability insurance, and fire insurance on contents, buildings, and property owned by the business

♦ Advertising and sales promotion costs

♦ Bad debts (credit sales never collected)

Many other specific operating expenses could be listed.

One reason for grouping all operating expenses (except depreciation) into one total account in the Income Statement is that the basic accounting for all these expenses can be explained in the same way. This chapter explains how operating expenses affect *Accounts Payable*. The next two chapters explain how operating expenses also affect two other Balance Sheet accounts.

It would be simple if every dollar of operating expenses charged to the year also were a dollar actually paid out in that same year. It would be nice and easy to equate operating expenses with cash disbursements; no other Balance Sheet (except Cash) would be affected by these expenses. But it's not quite that simple. Many operating expenses must be recorded *before* they are paid.

For example, on December 27 the company receives a bill from the utility company for power usage during the month period ending December 20. (Assume the company's accounting year ends December 31.) The amount of this expense clearly belongs in this year, so it is recorded in Accounts Payable.

This is just one example of many such unpaid operating expenses at the end of a company's accounting year. Other examples are bills from lawyers and CPAs for services, bills from newspapers for advertisements already run in the papers, telephone bills, and so on. Generally speaking, the credit terms of these payables are not long, 1 to 4 weeks being typical.

In this example we'll assume that the average credit period of the company's payables from unpaid operating expenses is 3 weeks. So, 3 weeks of its total operating expenses for the year are in Accounts Payable at year-end. In this example the average amount of operating expenses per week is $29,294 ($1,523,288 operating expenses for year ÷ 52 weeks = $29,294).

The amount of Accounts Payable at year-end from operating expenses is computed as follows:

$29,294   ×   3 weeks average   = $87, 882
Operating Expenses   credit period   Accounts
per week   Payable

See in Exhibit D that this amount is included in Accounts Payable.

Recall that inventory purchases on credit are also recorded in Accounts Payable. This liability account thus has a total balance of $388,834 at year-end ($300,952 from inventory purchases + $87,882 from operating expenses).

Every bill (or invoice) for goods or services received by the business is recorded in Accounts Payable. The immediate recording of these bills is necessary to recognize the liability and to recognize the increase of inventory or the increase of operating expense. However, the recording of these payables does *not* decrease Cash; there is no cash outflow. This very important point is discussed in Chapter 14, which deals with the cash flow analysis of profit.

INCOME STATEMENT FOR YEAR

Sales Revenue	$6,019,040
Cost of Goods Sold Expense	$3,912,376
Gross Margin	$2,106,664
Operating Expenses	$1,523,288
Operating Earnings Before Depreciation	$ 583,376
Depreciation Expense	$ 112,792
Operating Earnings	$ 470,584
Interest Expense	$ 76,650
Earnings Before Income Tax	$ 393,934
Income Tax Expense	$ 133,938
Net Income	$ 259,996

BALANCE SHEET AT END OF

Assets	This Year	Last Year
Cash	$ 256,663	$ 312,930
Accounts Receivable	$ 578,754	$ 482,350
Inventory	$ 978,094	$ 827,613
Prepaid Expenses	$ 117,176	$ 92,835
Total Current Assets	$1,930,687	$1,715,728
Property, Plant & Equipment	$1,986,450	$1,597,050
Accumulated Depreciation	($452,140)	($339,348)
Total Assets	$3,464,997	$2,973,430

Liabilities & Owners' Equity	This Year	Last Year
Accounts Payable:		
Inventory	$ 300,952	$ 268,300
Operating Expenses	$ 87,882	$ 62,216
Total	$ 388,834	$ 330,516
Accrued Expenses:		
Operations	$ 175,764	$ 137,900
Interest	$ 12,775	$ 10,356
Total	$ 188,539	$ 148,256
Income Tax Payable	$ 13,394	$ 11,674
Short-Term Notes Payable	$ 425,000	$ 375,000
Total Current Liabilities	$1,015,767	$ 865,446
Long-Term Notes Payable	$ 550,000	$ 475,000
Owners' Equity:		
Capital Stock	$ 725,000	$ 625,000
Retained Earnings	$1,174,230	$1,007,984
Total	$1,899,230	$1,632,984
Total Liabilities & Owners' Equity	$3,464,997	$2,973,430

CASH FLOW STATEMENT FOR YEAR

Cash Flows From Operating Activities		
Net Income		$259,996
Changes in Operating Cycle Assets and Liabilities:		
Accounts Receivable Increase	($96,404)	
Inventory Increase	($150,481)	
Prepaid Expenses Increase	($24,341)	
Accounts Payable Increase	$ 58,318	
Accrued Expenses Increase	$ 40,283	
Income Tax Payable Increase	$ 1,720	($170,905)
Operating Cash Flow, Before Depreciation		$ 89,091
Depreciation Expense		$112,792
Cash Flow From Profit-Making Operations		$201,883
Cash Flows From Investing Activities		
Purchases of Property, Plant & Equipment		($389,400)
Cash Flows From Financing Activities		
Net Increase in Short-Term Debt	$ 50,000	
Long-Term Borrowings	$ 75,000	
Capital Stock Issue	$100,000	
Cash Dividends To Stockholders	($93,750)	$131,250
Increase (Decrease) In Cash During Year		($56,267)

8

OPERATING EXPENSES
↓
ACCRUED EXPENSES (PAYABLE)

Refer to the connection in Exhibit D—Chapter 8 linking Operating Expenses in the Income Statement with Accrued Expenses in the Balance Sheet.

Now let's return to the utility expense example discussed in Chapter 7. Clearly, the utility cost through December 20 should be recorded in expense for the year. The utilities have been used in the operations of the business, and an actual bill has been received that is a clear and definite liability of the business. Now what about the utility usage from December 20 through December 31? The cost of utility usage for this last third of the month has not yet been billed to the business, nor even measured by the utility company, for that matter.

The accountant estimates the amount of this expense for the last third of December and records this amount so that total operating expenses include the full amount for the entire year. However, by December 31 no bill had been received from the utility company. The company had a liability for sure—an *unbilled* liability. So a different type of liability is recorded, called *Accrued Expenses*.

The Accrued Expenses liability is separated from Accounts Payable for two reasons. First, the amounts recorded in the Accrued Expenses liability are *estimates*, which depend on the methods and reliability of the methods used to make the estimates. In contrast, the amounts recorded in Accounts Payable are definite amounts. Second, the Accounts Payable are actual bills (invoices) in the hands of the company; Accrued Expenses are liabilities for which no bills have been received.

What are some of the estimated liabilities recorded in Accrued Expenses? More than you probably would guess. In addition to the utility expense example discussed above, the Accrued Expenses liability usually includes the following:

♦ Accumulated vacation and sick leave pay earned by employees, which has not yet been paid by the company; this can add up to a sizable amount

♦ Unpaid sales commissions earned by the company's salespersons that will be paid later

♦ Portions of annual property taxes that should be charged to this year that haven't been billed to the company yet

♦ Partial-month telephone costs that have been incurred but not yet billed to the company at year-end

In summary, about a third-month of utility cost, perhaps a half-month of telephone cost, maybe a half-year of employees' vacation cost, and several other such accumulated expenses are recorded in the Accrued Expenses at the end of the year. Not recording these liabilities would have caused a serious error in the profit measure for the year. Moreover, these are real liabilities, even though the amounts are estimated and no bills have been received.

In this example the average time before paying these liabilities is assumed to be 6 weeks. In other words, 6 weeks of its annual operating expenses are in Accrued Expenses at year-end. As computed in Chapter 7, the average operating expenses per week is $29,294 (see page 34). So the amount of Accrued Expenses from operating expenses is computed as follows:

$29,294   ×   6 weeks   = $175,764
Operating Expenses   average credit   Accrued
per week   period   Expenses

See in Exhibit D—Chapter 8 that the Accrued Expenses balance equals this amount.

The Accrued Expenses amount relative to total annual operating expenses may be more or less than 6 weeks for another business. Experience provides the guideline for each individual business. For many businesses 6 weeks is about right, even though this ratio may look rather high, especially if we consider both the Accrued Expenses (estimated unbilled liabilities) and Accounts Payable (definite billed liabilities). In Chapter 7 we see that 3 weeks of our company's total annual operating expenses are in Accounts Payable at year-end, and in this chapter we see that 6 weeks are in Accrued Expenses at year-end.

In summary, 9 weeks of the company's total operating expenses for the year are unpaid at year-end, which relieved the company of having to come up with this much cash for operating expenses during the year. The company avoided $263,646 of cash payout during the year ($87,882 Accounts Payable plus $175,764 Accrued Expenses).

If the company could have stretched the average wait (or credit period) for paying its operating expenses from 9 weeks to, say, 11 weeks, it could have avoided an additional $58,588 of cash disbursements ($29,294 average operating expenses per week × 2 additional weeks of waiting to pay the expenses = $58,588). So the Accounts Payable and Accrued Expenses resulting from operating expenses have a significant impact on cash flow. Any change in the size of these two liabilities relative to annual operating expenses has a cash flow impact that should not be ignored by the company's managers, as well as the creditors and investors who use its financial statements.

In Exhibit D you probably have noticed that there is another, though much smaller, source of Accrued Expenses—that is, the unpaid interest expense at year-end. This is discussed in Chapter 11.

Accrued Expenses and Accounts Payable result from the normal delay in paying for operating expenses. The expense is recorded now but paid for later; the liability bridges the two dates. In contrast, some expenses are paid for now but not recorded as an expense (deduction against sales revenue) until later. This reverse situation is discussed in the next chapter.

INCOME STATEMENT FOR YEAR

Sales Revenue	$6,019,040
Cost of Goods Sold Expense	$3,912,376
Gross Margin	$2,106,664
Operating Expenses	$1,523,288
Operating Earnings Before Depreciation	$ 583,376
Depreciation Expense	$ 112,792
Operating Earnings	$ 470,584
Interest Expense	$ 76,650
Earnings Before Income Tax	$ 393,934
Income Tax Expense	$ 133,938
Net Income	$ 259,996

BALANCE SHEET AT END OF

Assets	This Year	Last Year
Cash	$ 256,663	$ 312,930
Accounts Receivable	$ 578,754	$ 482,350
Inventory	$ 978,094	$ 827,613
Prepaid Expenses	$ 117,176	$ 92,835
Total Current Assets	$1,930,687	$1,715,728
Property, Plant & Equipment	$1,986,450	$1,597,050
Accumulated Depreciation	($452,140)	($339,348)
Total Assets	$3,464,997	$2,973,430

Liabilities & Owners' Equity	This Year	Last Year
Accounts Payable:		
Inventory	$ 300,952	$ 268,300
Operating Expenses	$ 87,882	$ 62,216
Total	$ 388,834	$ 330,516
Accrued Expenses:		
Operations	$ 175,764	$ 137,900
Interest	$ 12,775	$ 10,356
Total	$ 188,539	$ 148,256
Income Tax Payable	$ 13,394	$ 11,674
Short-Term Notes Payable	$ 425,000	$ 375,000
Total Current Liabilities	$1,015,767	$ 865,446
Long-Term Notes Payable	$ 550,000	$ 475,000
Owners' Equity:		
Capital Stock	$ 725,000	$ 625,000
Retained Earnings	$1,174,230	$1,007,984
Total	$1,899,230	$1,632,984
Total Liabilities & Owners' Equity	$3,464,997	$2,973,430

CASH FLOW STATEMENT FOR YEAR

Cash Flows From Operating Activities

Net Income		$259,996
Changes in Operating Cycle Assets and Liabilities:		
Accounts Receivable Increase	($96,404)	
Inventory Increase	($150,481)	
Prepaid Expenses Increase	($24,341)	
Accounts Payable Increase	$ 58,318	
Accrued Expenses Increase	$ 40,283	
Income Tax Payable Increase	$ 1,720	($170,905)
Operating Cash Flow, Before Depreciation		$ 89,091
Depreciation Expense		$112,792
Cash Flow From Profit-Making Operations		$201,883

Cash Flows From Investing Activities

Purchases of Property, Plant & Equipment		($389,400)

Cash Flows From Financing Activities

Net Increase in Short-Term Debt	$ 50,000	
Long-Term Borrowings	$ 75,000	
Capital Stock Issue	$100,000	
Cash Dividends To Stockholders	($93,750)	$131,250
Increase (Decrease) In Cash During Year		($56,267)

9

OPERATING EXPENSES

PREPAID EXPENSES

To begin, refer to the connection in Exhibit D—Chapter 9 linking Operating Expenses in the Income Statement with Prepaid Expenses in the Balance Sheet. The title of the chapter means that certain operating expenses cause Prepaid Expenses to appear in the Balance Sheet. However, the actual sequence of events is that certain operating costs are first paid in advance (prepaid), and then not until later are they charged off to expense.

Several operating costs must be paid for *before* these costs should be recorded as expense. There is a cash outlay before the amount should be recorded as an expense (as a deduction against sales revenue to measure profit for the period). For example, insurance premiums must be paid in advance of the insurance policy period. Office supplies are bought in quantities that last 2 to 3 months. Annual property taxes frequently are paid at the start of the tax assessment year. There are many more such examples of what are called *Prepaid Expenses*.

When paid, the cost is initially recorded in Prepaid Expenses, which is an asset account. The amount is allocated so that each future month receives its "fair share" of the cost.

Each month the appropriate part of the cost is taken out of Prepaid Expenses and recorded in expense. All of the costs initially recorded in Prepaid Expenses are later taken out and put in expense in the correct months.

Based on its experience and operations, a company can determine how large, on average, its Prepaid Expenses balance is relative to its annual operating expenses. We'll assume that the company's Prepaid Expenses in this example equal 4 weeks of its annual operating expenses. Previously (page 34) we computed that the operating expenses per week are $29,294. So the Prepaid Expenses balance is computed as follows:

$$\$29,294 \quad \times \quad 4 \text{ weeks} \quad = \quad \$117,176$$

$29,294	×	4 weeks	=	$117,176
Operating				Prepaid Expenses
Expenses				
per week				

See in Exhibit D that $117,176 is the balance of the Prepaid Expenses account.

In summary, the company in the example had to prepay one month of its annual operating expenses. This is a demand on cash during the year, in the amount of $117,176. If the manager could have reduced these prepayments to, say, only 3 weeks of the annual operating expenses (instead of 4 weeks in the example), the Prepaid Expenses would have been only $87,882 ($29,294 operating expenses per week $\times$ 3 weeks = $87,882). This would have reduced the demand on cash by $29,294, or one week of operating expenses.

On the other hand, if prepayments had been 3 weeks higher, say 7 weeks instead of 4 weeks in the example, the cash demand would have been $87,882 more. The cash flow impact of Prepaid Expenses is explained further in Chapter 14.

INCOME STATEMENT FOR YEAR

Sales Revenue	$6,019,040
Cost of Goods Sold Expense	$3,912,376
Gross Margin	$2,106,664
Operating Expenses	$1,523,288
Operating Earnings Before Depreciation	$ 583,376
Depreciation Expense	$ 112,792
Operating Earnings	$ 470,584
Interest Expense	$ 76,650
Earnings Before Income Tax	$ 393,934
Income Tax Expense	$ 133,938
Net Income	$ 259,996

BALANCE SHEET AT END OF

Assets	This Year	Last Year
Cash	$ 256,663	$ 312,930
Accounts Receivable	$ 578,754	$ 482,350
Inventory	$ 978,094	$ 827,613
Prepaid Expenses	$ 117,176	$ 92,835
Total Current Assets	$1,930,687	$1,715,728
Property, Plant & Equipment	$1,986,450	$1,597,050
Accumulated Depreciation	($452,140)	($339,348)
Total Assets	$3,464,997	$2,973,430

Liabilities & Owners' Equity	This Year	Last Year
Accounts Payable:		
Inventory	$ 300,952	$ 268,300
Operating Expenses	$ 87,882	$ 62,216
Total	$ 388,834	$ 330,516
Accrued Expenses:		
Operations	$ 175,764	$ 137,900
Interest	$ 12,775	$ 10,356
Total	$ 188,539	$ 148,256
Income Tax Payable	$ 13,394	$ 11,674
Short-Term Notes Payable	$ 425,000	$ 375,000
Total Current Liabilities	$1,015,767	$ 865,446
Long-Term Notes Payable	$ 550,000	$ 475,000
Owners' Equity:		
Capital Stock	$ 725,000	$ 625,000
Retained Earnings	$1,174,230	$1,007,984
Total	$1,899,230	$1,632,984
Total Liabilities & Owners' Equity	$3,464,997	$2,973,430

CASH FLOW STATEMENT FOR YEAR

Cash Flows From Operating Activities		
Net Income		$259,996
Changes in Operating Cycle Assets and Liabilities:		
Accounts Receivable Increase	($96,404)	
Inventory Increase	($150,481)	
Prepaid Expenses Increase	($24,341)	
Accounts Payable Increase	$ 58,318	
Accrued Expenses Increase	$ 40,283	
Income Tax Payable Increase	$ 1,720	($170,905)
Operating Cash Flow, Before Depreciation		$ 89,091
Depreciation Expense		$112,792
Cash Flow From Profit-Making Operations		$201,883
Cash Flows From Investing Activities		
Purchases of Property, Plant & Equipment		($389,400)
Cash Flows From Financing Activities		
Net Increase in Short-Term Debt	$ 50,000	
Long-Term Borrowings	$ 75,000	
Capital Stock Issue	$100,000	
Cash Dividends To Stockholders	($93,750)	$131,250
Increase (Decrease) In Cash During Year		($56,267)

10

PROPERTY, PLANT & EQUIPMENT
↓

DEPRECIATION
↓

ACCUMULATED DEPRECIATION

A Brief Review of Expense Accounting

By now you should have sensed the basic logic of expense accounting. Expenses are not necessarily recorded when they happen to be paid; expenses are not recorded on a cash basis. Expenses are recorded either on a *matching of costs with sales revenues* basis or on a *cost of period* basis. Each basis is explained briefly here:

1. *Matching of costs with sales revenue basis*—cost of goods sold expense, sales commissions expense, and all other expenses directly identifiable with making sales are recorded in the same period as the sales revenue. The purpose is to match these costs with related sales revenue to get the correct measure of profit from sales.

2. *Cost of period basis*—many expenses are not directly identifiable with particular sales, such as office employees' salaries, rent of building space, data processing and record-keeping, legal and audit, insurance, interest on borrowed money, and many more. Nondirect expenses are just as necessary as direct expenses. But there is no objective way to match them with individual sales. So the nondirect expenses are recorded in the period in which benefit or use to the operations of the business takes place. For example, $1/12$ of the annual fire insurance premium is allocated to each month, office supplies are expensed in the month used, and so on.

The timing of expense recordings for the purpose of matching the expense with the correct sales revenue or matching the expense in the correct time period involves the use of asset and liability accounts. We have already discussed the use of Inventory and Prepaid Expenses for this purpose, as well as the Accounts Payable and Accrued Expenses liabilities. One type of asset not yet discussed is *Property, Plant & Equipment*, which we now turn to.

Depreciation Expense

In this example the company owns its real estate (land and buildings), as well as the other long-lived assets needed in its operations. For example, this company owns desks, cash registers, a computer system, trucks, display cabinets, shelving, various machines and tools, and so on.

These several different assets are grouped together under the heading Property, Plant & Equipment, which has a balance of $1,986,450 at the end of the most recent year. Please see Exhibit D—Chapter 10.

You may also want to refer to Exhibit B on page 9 again, which shows the classified Balance Sheet of the company. Notice that in the Balance Sheet these assets are reported in a more descriptive account called *Land, Building, Machines, Equipment and Furniture*, which is positioned under the Property, Plant & Equipment heading.

Long-lived operating assets are used several years, but eventually they wear out or otherwise lose their usefulness to the business. In short, these assets have a limited life span of business (economic) usefulness. For instance, a typewriter will be disposed of sometime; it won't last forever.

The cost of the typewriter is prorated over each future year of expected use to the business. How many years? This is hardly more than an educated guess. As a practical matter the minimum, or shortest lives allowed for federal income tax purposes usually are the useful life estimates adopted by a business to depreciate its long-term operating assets in the financial statements.

The Tax Reform Act (TRA) of 1986 made major changes in allowable life estimates. Buildings have a useful life of 31.5 years. Cars and light trucks have 5-year useful lives. Most equipment and machinery fall in either the 7- or 10-years useful life category.

The logic of the tax law is based on the Accelerated Cost Recovery System (ACRS), which means that the business should recover the cost invested in its long-term operating assets by depreciating the cost of the assets over their useful lives.

"Accelerated" means that the tax law permits the assets to be depreciated faster than they actually wear out. For example, most buildings are still valuable after 31.5 years of use—though some might be torn down before then.

Accelerated also means that assets (except buildings) can be depreciated according to a front-end loading method whereby more depreciation is recorded in the earlier years than in the later years of the assets' useful lives.

In this example the total depreciation expense recorded in the most recent year of business is $112,792, which is based on the ACRS lives permitted by the tax law. See Exhibit D—Chapter 10 again; notice depreciation expense in the Income Statement of this amount. One major asset (its building) is depreciated by the straight-line method, whereas its other assets (trucks and equipment, for example) are depreciated according to an accelerated, or front-end loading method. Depreciation expense methods are discussed further in Chapter 22.

The amount of depreciation expense charged to each year is relatively arbitrary compared to other expenses. One reason is that the useful life estimates are arbitrary. For a 12-months' insurance policy, there's little doubt that the total premium cost should be allocated over exactly 12 months. But long-lived assets, such as office desks, display shelving, file cabinets, computers, or typewriters, present much more difficult problems. How long will these assets be used? Past experience is a guide but still leaves much room for error.

Given the inherent problems of estimating useful lives, financial statement readers are well advised to keep in mind the consequences of wrong estimates. If the useful life estimates are too short, depreciation expense each year is too high. In fact, useful life estimates are generally too short. Accountants, with the blessing of the Internal Revenue Code, take a very conservative approach. Rather than depreciate their assets one way for income tax and another way for their financial statements, most businesses use the income tax way for their financial reporting as well.

The Accumulated Depreciation Account

The amount of depreciation expense each year is not recorded as a decrease in the asset account directly. Instead, each year the amount of depreciation expense is added to the Accumulated Depreciation account. The balance in this account is deducted from the original cost of the assets (see Exhibit B, page 9). The remainder—$1,534,310 in this example—is called the *book value*. It's the undepreciated part of the assets' original cost, or future depreciation expense if you would.

The Accumulated Depreciation balance ($452,140 from Exhibit D—Chapter 10) is the total depreciation recorded in this and previous years. There is no way to tell how much of the balance was recorded last year, or the year before that, and so on. Putting it a different way, businesses do not have to report the average age of their long-term operating assets.

Book Values of Long-Lived Assets
Compared with Their Replacement Costs

After several years the original cost of the long-lived assets reported in a company's Balance Sheet may be quite low compared to the current replacement costs of equivalent new long-lived assets. Inflation has hit these asset costs as much or more than everything else. The original cost amounts reported in a Balance Sheet are not meant to be indicators of the current replacement costs of the assets.

When looking ahead, managers, creditors, and investors should realize that the future replacement costs of these assets may be much higher than the historical costs reported in the Balance Sheet. For management purposes, every year or two it's a good idea to make an estimate of the current replacement costs of the business' long-lived operating assets. This does not and should not lead to a write-up of the assets in the Balance Sheet. This would be against generally accepted accounting principles.

Many business managers and many accountants have argued that such assets should be written up once every year to keep up with inflation, and that the depreciation expense each year should be based on the higher values. So far Congress has rejected this method for federal income tax purposes.

Nevertheless, the matter has been one of very serious and continuing concern to the accounting profession, even though many doubt the usefulness of such information to investors. Somewhat as an experiment, the rule-making body of the accounting profession several years ago passed a requirement that large (indeed, very large!) public corporations must provide *supplementary* information about the current costs of their long-lived operating assets. However, this requirement was later repealed.

The replacement cost argument for reporting long-term operating assets and for recording depreciation expense has many die-hard advocates. Every now and then you see criticism of financial accounting on the grounds that depreciation expense is based on historical cost. Few take it seriously, unless they would think Congress might allow replacement cost depreciation to determine taxable income. Not very likely, in my opinion.

INCOME STATEMENT FOR YEAR

Sales Revenue	$6,019,040
Cost of Goods Sold Expense	$3,912,376
Gross Margin	$2,106,664
Operating Expenses	$1,523,288
Operating Earnings Before Depreciation	$ 583,376
Depreciation Expense	$ 112,792
Operating Earnings	$ 470,584
Interest Expense	$ 76,650
Earnings Before Income Tax	$ 393,934
Income Tax Expense	$ 133,938
Net Income	$ 259,996

BALANCE SHEET AT END OF

Assets	This Year	Last Year
Cash	$ 256,663	$ 312,930
Accounts Receivable	$ 578,754	$ 482,350
Inventory	$ 978,094	$ 827,613
Prepaid Expenses	$ 117,176	$ 92,835
Total Current Assets	$1,930,687	$1,715,728
Property, Plant & Equipment	$1,986,450	$1,597,050
Accumulated Depreciation	($452,140)	($339,348)
Total Assets	$3,464,997	$2,973,430

Liabilities & Owners' Equity	This Year	Last Year
Accounts Payable:		
Inventory	$ 300,952	$ 268,300
Operating Expenses	$ 87,882	$ 62,216
Total	$ 388,834	$ 330,516
Accrued Expenses:		
Operations	$ 175,764	$ 137,900
Interest	$ 12,775	$ 10,356
Total	$ 188,539	$ 148,256
Income Tax Payable	$ 13,394	$ 11,674
Short-Term Notes Payable	$ 425,000	$ 375,000
Total Current Liabilities	$1,015,767	$ 865,446
Long-Term Notes Payable	$ 550,000	$ 475,000
Owners' Equity:		
Capital Stock	$ 725,000	$ 625,000
Retained Earnings	$1,174,230	$1,007,984
Total	$1,899,230	$1,632,984
Total Liabilities & Owners' Equity	$3,464,997	$2,973,430

CASH FLOW STATEMENT FOR YEAR

Cash Flows From Operating Activities		
Net Income		$259,996
Changes in Operating Cycle Assets and Liabilities:		
Accounts Receivable Increase	($96,404)	
Inventory Increase	($150,481)	
Prepaid Expenses Increase	($24,341)	
Accounts Payable Increase	$ 58,318	
Accrued Expenses Increase	$ 40,283	
Income Tax Payable Increase	$ 1,720	($170,905)
Operating Cash Flow, Before Depreciation		$ 89,091
Depreciation Expense		$112,792
Cash Flow From Profit-Making Operations		$201,883
Cash Flows From Investing Activities		
Purchases of Property, Plant & Equipment		($389,400)
Cash Flows From Financing Activities		
Net Increase in Short-Term Debt	$ 50,000	
Long-Term Borrowings	$ 75,000	
Capital Stock Issue	$100,000	
Cash Dividends To Stockholders	($93,750)	$131,250
Increase (Decrease) In Cash During Year		(56,267)

11

INTEREST EXPENSE

$\downarrow$

ACCRUED EXPENSES (PAYABLE)

It's a rare business that doesn't borrow money, in addition to having Accounts Payable and Accrued Expenses liabilities. A *note* (or similar legal instrument) is signed when borrowing; hence the liabilities from borrowing are called *Notes Payable*. One main difference is that interest is paid on borrowed money of course, whereas no interest is paid on Accounts Payable and Accrued Expenses. Notes Payable are always reported separately from non-interest-bearing liabilities in the Balance Sheet.

Interest is a charge per day for the use of borrowed money. Every day the money is borrowed means that more interest is owed. The ratio of interest to the amount borrowed is called the interest rate, and always is stated as a percent. Percent means "per hundred." If you borrow $100,000 for one year and pay $8,000 interest, the rate (ratio) of interest is: $8,000 interest ÷ $100,000 borrowed = $8 per $100, or 8%. Interest rates are stated as annual rates, even if the term of borrowing is shorter or longer than 1 year.

Interest is reported as a separate expense in the Income Statement. It's not the size of interest relative to other expenses, but its special nature that requires this separate disclosure. Interest is a financial cost as opposed to an operating cost; interest depends on the financial policies of the business regarding borrowing, not on its methods of operations.

When interest is paid *depends*. On short-term notes (less than 1-year periods) interest is paid in one sum at the maturity date of the note, which is the last day of the loan period. On longer-term notes, say for 5 or 10 years, interest is paid usually every 6 months, although monthly or quarterly interest payments are not unheard of. On both short-term and long-term notes there is a lag, or delay, in paying interest. But the interest expense should be recorded for all days the money was borrowed.

The accumulated amount of unpaid interest expense at the end of the accounting period is recorded in *Accrued Expenses*, which is a liability account. In this example the company's interest expense is $6,387.50 per month. Due to the lag in paying interest, 2 months expense is unpaid at year-end, so:

$6,387.50   ×   2 months   = $12,775
Interest Expense   Accrued Expenses
per month

See the connection in Exhibit D—Chapter 11.

You'll notice that Accrued Expenses now has a total balance of $188,539—the $12,775 unpaid interest expense plus the $175,764 unpaid operating expenses that were discussed earlier in Chapter 8.

INCOME STATEMENT FOR YEAR

Sales Revenue	$6,019,040
Cost of Goods Sold Expense	$3,912,376
Gross Margin	$2,106,664
Operating Expenses	$1,523,288
Operating Earnings Before Depreciation	$ 583,376
Depreciation Expense	$ 112,792
Operating Earnings	$ 470,584
Interest Expense	$ 76,650
Earnings Before Income Tax	$ 393,934
Income Tax Expense	$ 133,938
Net Income	$ 259,996

BALANCE SHEET AT END OF

Assets	This Year	Last Year
Cash	$ 256,663	$ 312,930
Accounts Receivable	$ 578,754	$ 482,350
Inventory	$ 978,094	$ 827,613
Prepaid Expenses	$ 117,176	$ 92,835
Total Current Assets	$1,930,687	$1,715,728
Property, Plant & Equipment	$1,986,450	$1,597,050
Accumulated Depreciation	($452,140)	($339,348)
Total Assets	$3,464,997	$2,973,430

Liabilities & Owners' Equity	This Year	Last Year
Accounts Payable:		
Inventory	$ 300,952	$ 268,300
Operating Expenses	$ 87,882	$ 62,216
Total	$ 388,834	$ 330,516
Accrued Expenses:		
Operations	$ 175,764	$ 137,900
Interest	$ 12,775	$ 10,356
Total	$ 188,539	$ 148,256
Income Tax Payable	$ 13,394	$ 11,674
Short-Term Notes Payable	$ 425,000	$ 375,000
Total Current Liabilities	$1,015,767	$ 865,446
Long-Term Notes Payable	$ 550,000	$ 475,000
Owners' Equity:		
Capital Stock	$ 725,000	$ 625,000
Retained Earnings	$1,174,230	$1,007,984
Total	$1,899,230	$1,632,984
Total Liabilities & Owners' Equity	$3,464,997	$2,973,430

CASH FLOW STATEMENT FOR YEAR

Cash Flows From Operating Activities

Net Income		$259,996
Changes in Operating Cycle Assets and Liabilities:		
Accounts Receivable Increase	($96,404)	
Inventory Increase	($150,481)	
Prepaid Expenses Increase	($24,341)	
Accounts Payable Increase	$ 58,318	
Accrued Expenses Increase	$ 40,283	
Income Tax Payable Increase	$ 1,720	($170,905)
Operating Cash Flow, Before Depreciation		$ 89,091
Depreciation Expense		$112,792
Cash Flow From Profit-Making Operations		$201,883

Cash Flows From Investing Activities

Purchases of Property, Plant & Equipment		($389,400)

Cash Flows From Financing Activities

Net Increase in Short-Term Debt	$ 50,000	
Long-Term Borrowings	$ 75,000	
Capital Stock Issue	$100,000	
Cash Dividends To Stockholders	($93,750)	$131,250
Increase (Decrease) In Cash During Year		($56,267)

12

INCOME TAX EXPENSE
↓
INCOME TAX PAYABLE

Refer to the connection in Exhibit D—Chapter 12 between Income Tax Expense in the Income Statement with Income Tax Payable in the Balance Sheet.

The business in our example is incorporated. A corporation, being a separate entity (person) in the eyes of the law, has several legal advantages. However, profit-motivated business corporations have one serious disadvantage—they are subject to federal and state income taxes as a separate entity.

The term "subject to" here is used deliberately. First, a corporation must earn a taxable income to be taxed. Second, there are many provisions and options in the tax laws that result in paying less tax, or perhaps no income tax at all, in a given year.

It takes hundreds of pages in the federal law to define *taxable income*. Then it takes many more pages to define how to compute the income tax owed on the amount of taxable income. The 1986 Tax Reform Act, for one thing, reinforced the rules regarding the Alternative Minimum Tax (AMT) to better control the avoidance of income tax. Surely you know how complex is the federal income tax on business corporations (as well as individuals). Also, most states impose an income tax on corporations doing business in their boundaries.

This is not the place to explain taxation of business profit. To simplify, therefore, two key assumptions are made in this example.

First Simplifying Assumption

The company's accounting methods used to determine its annual taxable income are the same methods used to prepare its financial statements. There are no differences in recording its sales revenue and no differences in recording its expenses. Also, it is assumed that all recorded expenses are fully deductible for income tax purposes. Generally speaking, this harmony of income tax and financial statement accounting methods is true. Yet, many differences are permitted. To minimize its taxable income, a corporation may use more conservative accounting methods in its tax returns than in its financial statements. This would lead us into very technical and complex detours from the main discussion.

Second Simplifying Assumption

In this example the federal income rate is a flat 34%, and there is no state income tax. This avoids several tax computation steps. For instance, reduced federal tax rates apply on the taxable income layers below $100,001; and, state tax is deductible for federal purposes and federal tax is deductible for state purposes.

Given these two assumptions, the corporation's taxable income is $393,934 (see Exhibit D—Chapter 12), and its total income tax for the year is:

$393,934	× 34%	= $133,938
Taxable Income	Federal Income Tax Rate	Income Tax Expense for year

Corporations have to make progress payments on their income tax as they go through the year. Simply speaking, at the start of the year a corporation makes an estimate of what its taxable income will be for the coming year. Based on this estimated taxable income, the corporation estimates its income tax for the year. The corporation has to make installment payments during the year, totaling 90% of its estimated tax for the year.

If less than 90% is paid during the year, penalties on the amount of underpayment may be imposed. However, there are several technical provisions and exceptions that may come into play such that the business escapes any penalty. It is not unrealistic to assume that a business paid in less than 90% during the year. However, we'll assume that the business in this example paid 90% and thus 10% is still owed to the Internal Revenue Service at year-end:

See the connection in Exhibit D—Chapter 12.

$133,938   × 10% balance   = $13,394
Income Tax   owed on total   Income Tax
Expense for year income tax   Payable
                  for the year

BALANCE SHEET AT END OF

INCOME STATEMENT FOR YEAR	
Sales Revenue	$6,019,040
Cost of Goods Sold Expense	$3,912,376
Gross Margin	$2,106,664
Operating Expenses	$1,523,288
Operating Earnings Before Depreciation	$ 583,376
Depreciation Expense	$ 112,792
Operating Earnings	$ 470,584
Interest Expense	$ 76,650
Earnings Before Income Tax	$ 393,934
Income Tax Expense	$ 133,938
Net Income	$ 259,996

Assets	This Year	Last Year
Cash	$ 256,663	$ 312,930
Accounts Receivable	$ 578,754	$ 482,350
Inventory	$ 978,094	$ 827,613
Prepaid Expenses	$ 117,176	$ 92,835
Total Current Assets	$1,930,687	$1,715,728
Property, Plant & Equipment	$1,986,450	$1,597,050
Accumulated Depreciation	($452,140)	($339,348)
Total Assets	$3,464,997	$2,973,430

Liabilities & Owners' Equity	This Year	Last Year
Accounts Payable:		
Inventory	$ 300,952	$ 268,300
Operating Expenses	$ 87,882	$ 62,216
Total	$ 388,834	$ 330,516
Accrued Expenses:		
Operations	$ 175,764	$ 137,900
Interest	$ 12,775	$ 10,356
Total	$ 188,539	$ 148,256
Income Tax Payable	$ 13,394	$ 11,674
Short-Term Notes Payable	$ 425,000	$ 375,000
Total Current Liabilities	$1,015,767	$ 865,446
Long-Term Notes Payable	$ 550,000	$ 475,000
Owners' Equity:		
Capital Stock	$ 725,000	$ 625,000
Retained Earnings	$1,174,230	$1,007,984
Total	$1,899,230	$1,632,984
Total Liabilities & Owners' Equity	$3,464,997	$2,973,430

CASH FLOW STATEMENT FOR YEAR

Cash Flows From Operating Activities		
Net Income		$259,996
Changes in Operating Cycle Assets and Liabilities:		
Accounts Receivable Increase	($96,404)	
Inventory Increase	($150,481)	
Prepaid Expenses Increase	($24,341)	
Accounts Payable Increase	$ 58,318	
Accrued Expenses Increase	$ 40,283	
Income Tax Payable Increase	$ 1,720	($170,905)
Operating Cash Flow, Before Depreciation		$ 89,091
Depreciation Expense		$112,792
Cash Flow From Profit-Making Operations		$201,883
Cash Flows From Investing Activities		
Purchases of Property, Plant & Equipment		($389,400)
Cash Flows From Financing Activities		
Net Increase in Short-Term Debt	$ 50,000	
Long-Term Borrowings	$ 75,000	
Capital Stock Issue	$100,000	
Cash Dividends To Stockholders	($93,750)	$131,250
Increase (Decrease) In Cash During Year		($56,267)

13

NET INCOME (PROFIT)
↓
RETAINED EARNINGS

See the connection in Exhibit D—Chapter 13 linking Net Income from the Income Statement to Retained Earnings in the Balance Sheet. Net income increases the balance in the Retained Earnings account. As explained before, but worth repeating here, net income is the final profit after deducting all expenses from sales revenue.

Now a very important question: At year-end, where is net income? The answer to this question requires that we build on the discussion in previous chapters. Sales revenue results in asset increases, and expenses result in asset decreases or liability increases. Sales revenue and expenses affect virtually all the assets and most of the liabilities of a business, as explained in previous chapters.

Profit means that the company's net assets (assets less liabilities) must have increased during the period. Exhibit E summarizes the increases and decreases in the company's operating assets and operating liabilities resulting from its profit for the year, i.e., from its sales revenue and expenses. The decrease in the Property, Plant & Equipment account is the depreciation expense for the year. Except for the Cash account the other increases are determined by comparing the ending balance with the beginning balance for each account in the Balance Sheet in Exhibit D—Chapter 13.

The Cash increase shown in Exhibit E is the increase caused by the company's profit-making operations for the year. There were other non-profit sources and uses of cash during the year, so Cash did not increase by the $201,883* shown in Exhibit E.

*God forbid, but occasionally you still see the term "Earned Surplus" (instead of Retained Earnings). This title is especially confusing and as outmoded as the Model T.

The next two chapters explain the cash flow analysis of profit in more detail, and other sources and uses of cash. The main point here is that net income consists of a mix of increases and decreases in several operating asset and liability accounts. Net income is not simply money added to the company's bank account. Dividends, if and when paid, are recorded as decreases in Retained Earnings, which is explained in Chapter 15.

In short, the balance in Retained Earnings is just that—the amount of net income earned *and* retained by the business. Sometimes it's called Undistributed Net Income, or

EXHIBIT E - ASSET AND LIABILITY CHANGES CAUSED BY NET INCOME, OR SALES REVENUE AND EXPENSE OPERATIONS

Asset Changes

Cash	+$201,883	
Accounts Receivable	+ 96,404	
Inventory	+ 150,481	
Prepaid Expenses	+ 24,341	
Property, Plant & Equipment	− 112,792	
Total Asset Increases		$360,317

Liability Changes

Accounts Payable	+$ 58,318	
Accrued Expenses	+ 40,283	
Income Tax Payable	+ 1,720	
Total Liability Increases		$100,321
Net Income (Asset Increases less Liability Increases)		$259,996

Undistributed Earnings, though the title Retained Earnings is much more common.*

It's very important to understand that Retained Earnings is *not* an asset. Nor does it indicate how much cash or how much of any other particular asset the company has. Think of Retained Earnings as a balance account, the last weight you put on the scales to make for a perfect balance.

Let's return to Exhibit E again, which summarizes the asset and liability changes from net income for the year. To summarize even further, net income can be put as follows:

$360,317	− $100,321	= $259,996
Increases in assets	Increases in liabilities	Net income

Without Retained Earnings in the Balance Sheet, net income would cause an imbalance, like a teeter-totter out of balance:

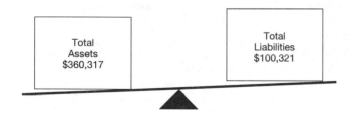

With Retained Earnings there is a balance:

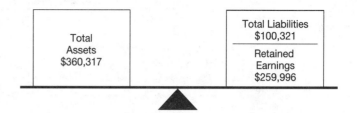

Retained Earnings does more than keep the Balance Sheet in a condition of equality. It keeps track of how much of total owners' (stockholders') equity was earned and retained by the business versus how much capital has been invested from time to time by the owners (which is recorded in the other owners' equity account). Legally these two sources of owners' equity must be separated.

Looking at the Retained Earnings balance is like looking into a mirror. The real profit earned by a business is found in the assets less the liabilities of the business. Retained Earnings is only the image in the mirror (in one amount).

		BALANCE SHEET AT END OF			CASH FLOW STATEMENT FOR YEAR	

INCOME STATEMENT FOR YEAR

Sales Revenue	$6,019,040
Cost of Goods Sold Expense	$3,912,376
Gross Margin	$2,106,664
Operating Expenses	$1,523,288
Operating Earnings Before Depreciation	$ 583,376
Depreciation Expense	$ 112,792
Operating Earnings	$ 470,584
Interest Expense	$ 76,650
Earnings Before Income Tax	$ 393,934
Income Tax Expense	$ 133,938
Net Income	$ 259,996

BALANCE SHEET AT END OF

Assets	This Year	Last Year
Cash	$ 256,663	$ 312,930
Accounts Receivable	$ 578,754	$ 482,350
Inventory	$ 978,094	$ 827,613
Prepaid Expenses	$ 117,176	$ 92,835
Total Current Assets	$1,930,687	$1,715,728
Property, Plant & Equipment	$1,986,450	$1,597,050
Accumulated Depreciation	($452,140)	($339,348)
Total Assets	$3,464,997	$2,973,430

Liabilities & Owners' Equity	This Year	Last Year
Accounts Payable:		
Inventory	$ 300,952	$ 268,300
Operating Expenses	$ 87,882	$ 62,216
Total	$ 388,834	$ 330,516
Accrued Expenses:		
Operations	$ 175,764	$ 137,900
Interest	$ 12,775	$ 10,356
Total	$ 188,539	$ 148,256
Income Tax Payable	$ 13,394	$ 11,674
Short-Term Notes Payable	$ 425,000	$ 375,000
Total Current Liabilities	$1,015,767	$ 865,446
Long-Term Notes Payable	$ 550,000	$ 475,000
Owners' Equity:		
Capital Stock	$ 725,000	$ 625,000
Retained Earnings	$1,174,230	$1,007,984
Total	$1,899,230	$1,632,984
Total Liabilities & Owners' Equity	$3,464,997	$2,973,430

CASH FLOW STATEMENT FOR YEAR

Cash Flows From Operating Activities

Net Income		$259,996
Changes in Operating Cycle Assets and Liabilities:		
Accounts Receivable Increase	($96,404)	
Inventory Increase	($150,481)	
Prepaid Expenses Increase	($24,341)	
Accounts Payable Increase	$ 58,318	
Accrued Expenses Increase	$ 40,283	
Income Tax Payable Increase	$ 1,720	($170,905)
Operating Cash Flow, Before Depreciation		$ 89,091
Depreciation Expense		$112,792
Cash Flow From Profit-Making Operations		$201,883

Cash Flows From Investing Activities

Purchases of Property, Plant & Equipment		($389,400)

Cash Flows From Financing Activities

Net Increase in Short-Term Debt	$ 50,000	
Long-Term Borrowings	$ 75,000	
Capital Stock Issue	$100,000	
Cash Dividends To Stockholders	($93,750)	$131,250
Increase (Decrease) In Cash During Year		($56,267)

14

CASH FLOW ANALYSIS
OF PROFIT

Making sales and controlling expenses is a demanding task, to say the least. However, earning an adequate profit is not enough. Managing cash is just as important. Enough cash must be available *when needed*. Earning a good profit does not necessarily guarantee an adequate cash flow when needed.

In short, business managers have a double duty: to earn profit, and to convert the profit into cash reasonably soon. Waiting too long to turn profit into cash reduces the value of the profit because of the time value of money.

Managers use the Income Statement to review and evaluate profit performance and to prepare the profit plan for the coming year. Likewise, managers should use the *Cash Flow Statement* to review cash flows for the year just ended and to prepare the cash flow budget for the coming year. Not to plan cash flows would invite disaster.

Exhibit D—Chapter 14 presents the company's Cash Flow Statement for its most recent year of business on the right side of its Balance Sheet. The top part of the Cash Flow statement, with the several lines of connection pointing into it, is discussed in this chapter; the remainder of the statement is discussed in Chapter 15.

The company's Cash Flow Statement begins with an analysis of the cash flow effects from operations, which are all those activities directly a part of making profit (net income). In other words, operations refers to those transactions of making sales and incurring expenses.

Net income is earned when sales revenue and expenses are recorded. These recordings, in large part, are made either before or after the related cash flows occur. Over a long time, say 10 to 15 years, the total increase in cash would be very close to the total net income earned. But in any one year the cash flow can be considerably less or more than the amount of net income reported in the Income Statement for that year.

Changes in a company's operating assets and operating liabilities during the year cause cash flow from its profit-making operations to be different than net income from its profit-making operations. Please see in Exhibit D—Chapter 14 the lines extending from the operating assets and operating liabilities into the Cash Flow Statement.

Accounts Receivable increased $96,404 during the year. The $482,350 carryover from the end of last year was collected during the early part of the year, which adds to the cash flow from sales revenue. However, the $578,754 at the end of the year was not collected, which takes away from the cash flow from sales revenue. The net effect is that the company took in $96,404 less cash than its sales for the year. So, the $96,404 Accounts Receivable increase is deducted from net income.

Inventory increased $150,481 during the year, from an opening balance of $827,613 at the start of the year (the ending balance from last year) to $978,094 at the end of this year. In addition to the cost of goods sold during the year the company built up its stock of goods held for sale by $150,481. From the cash flow point of view the company laid out $150,481 in addition to the cost of goods sold. So, the $150,481 Inventory increase is deducted from net income in the Cash Flow Statement.

Prepaid Expenses increased $24,341 during the year, from $92,835 at the end of last year to $117,176 at the end of this year. The $92,835 beginning balance was charged to Operating Expenses this year. But, the business did not have to pay this amount because these items were already paid for last year, which is why they are called "prepaid." In other words, cash outlays this year were relieved by the $92,835 prepaid last year.

However, $117,176 was paid out during this year that will not be charged to expense until next year, which is the ending balance of Prepaid Expenses. Cash was decreased even though there was no charge to Operating Expenses during the year. The net effect on cash flow is a negative $24,341, which is deducted from net income in the Cash Flow Statement.

To this point things don't look so good from the cash flow point of view. The three operating asset increases discussed so far cause a total *negative* cash flow impact of $271,226, which is more than net income for the year! However, on the other side of the coin, the company had positive cash flow effects from the increases of its operating liabilities.

Earlier chapters explain that three liabilities are directly affected by the expenses of the business—Accounts Payable, Accrued Expenses, and Income Tax Payable. All three increased during the year, as you can see from the comparative Balance Sheet in the middle of Exhibit D—Chapter 14. These liability amounts at the start of the year (i.e., the carryover ending balances from last year) were paid during the early months of the year.

In contrast, the ending balances of these liabilities are amounts that were not paid. Cash payments equal to these ending amounts were avoided during the year; cash will not be paid until next year. Thus, the increases in these three operating liabilities are added to net income in the Cash Flow Statement.

The positive cash flow effects of the three operating liabilities offset the negative cash flow effects of the three operating assets. The net amount of all six is a negative cash flow impact of $170,905 which is deducted from net income—as you can see in the Cash Flow Statement.

So, down to this point the operating cash flow before depreciation is only $89,091. The reasons for calculating this particular subtotal in the Cash Flow Statement is made clear later in Chapter 16, which explains the impact of growth and decline on cash flow. For now, we move on to depreciation.

Depreciation is not a cash outlay. As explained earlier in Chapter 10, depreciation is essentially a "write-down" of the long-term operating assets (Property, Plant & Equipment). Depreciation recognizes the gradual wear and tear and the relentless loss of economic usefulness of these assets to the business. No cash is paid out when recording depreciation expense. Indeed, cash was paid out years earlier when the assets were bought.

Depreciation expense is recorded as an increase in the Accumulated Depreciation account, which is a "contra account" that is deducted from the Property, Plant & Equipment asset account. The main point here is that the Cash account is not decreased. So, the $112,792 depreciation expense is added to net income.

In conclusion, the company's cash flow from its profit making operations is $201,883 for the year. In other words, profit generated $201,883 cash flow over the year. The company earned $259,996 profit over the year, but given the changes in its operating assets and operating liabilities its profit generated "only" $201,883 cash flow over the year. The two numbers should never be confused although the two are linked together, as the next section explains.

Reconciling the Cash Basis and Accrual Basis

By now I hope that I have made very clear that the Income Statement is reported on the accrual basis of accounting, which is absolutely necessary for measuring sales revenue and expenses to determine the profit (or loss) of a business. The company in our example earned $259,996 net income (i.e., profit) for its most recent year—see the Income Statement in Exhibit D—Chapter 14. It did not earn $201,883, which is the cash flow from profit.

The distinction between the cash basis and accrual basis is extraordinarily important. Exhibit F reconciles the differences between the two perspectives on the profit-making operations of the business. They are both correct; one looks at the cash flow effects of profit, whereas the other is the accounting basis by which profit is measured.

By the way, you might compare the cash basis amounts with the cash flows presented in Exhibit A at the start of the book (see page 3). They are the same amounts.

EXHIBIT F - ACCRUAL BASIS OF PROFIT MEASUREMENT RECONCILED WITH CASH FLOW BASIS

	Accrual Basis	Changes in Operating Assets and Liabilities	Cash Basis
Sales Revenue	$6,019,040	Less $96,404 Increase in Accounts Receivable	$5,922,636
Cost of goods sold expense	(3,912,376)	Plus $150,481 Increase in Inventory Less $32,652 Increase in Accounts Payable - Inventory	($4,030,205)
Operating expenses	(1,523,288)	Plus $24,341 Increase in Prepaid Expenses Less $25,666 Increase in Accounts Payable - Operating Expenses Less $37,864 Increase in Accrued Expenses - Operations	(1,484,099)
Depreciation expense	(112,792)	Less entire amount, which is not a cash outlay	0
Interest expense	(76,650)	Less $2,419 Increase in Accrued Expenses - Interest	(74,231)
Income tax expense	(133,938)	Less $1,720 Increase in Income Tax Payable	(132,218)
	$259,996 **Net Income**		$201,883 **Cash Flow From Profit**

INCOME STATEMENT FOR YEAR

Sales Revenue	$6,019,040
Cost of Goods Sold Expense	$3,912,376
Gross Margin	$2,106,664
Operating Expenses	$1,523,288
Operating Earnings Before Depreciation	$ 583,376
Depreciation Expense	$ 112,792
Operating Earnings	$ 470,584
Interest Expense	$ 76,650
Earnings Before Income Tax	$ 393,934
Income Tax Expense	$ 133,938
Net Income	$ 259,996

BALANCE SHEET AT END OF

Assets	This Year	Last Year
Cash	$ 256,663	$ 312,930
Accounts Receivable	$ 578,754	$ 482,350
Inventory	$ 978,094	$ 827,613
Prepaid Expenses	$ 117,176	$ 92,835
Total Current Assets	$1,930,687	$1,715,728
Property, Plant & Equipment	$1,986,450	$1,597,050
Accumulated Depreciation	($452,140)	($339,348)
Total Assets	$3,464,997	$2,973,430

Liabilities & Owners' Equity	This Year	Last Year
Accounts Payable:		
Inventory	$ 300,952	$ 268,300
Operating Expenses	$ 87,882	$ 62,216
Total	$ 388,834	$ 330,516
Accrued Expenses:		
Operations	$ 175,764	$ 137,900
Interest	$ 12,775	$ 10,356
Total	$ 188,539	$ 148,256
Income Tax Payable	$ 13,394	$ 11,674
Short-Term Notes Payable	$ 425,000	$ 375,000
Total Current Liabilities	$1,015,767	$ 865,446
Long-Term Notes Payable	$ 550,000	$ 475,000
Owners' Equity:		
Capital Stock	$ 725,000	$ 625,000
Retained Earnings	$1,174,230	$1,007,984
Total	$1,899,230	$1,632,984
Total Liabilities & Owners' Equity	$3,464,997	$2,973,430

CASH FLOW STATEMENT FOR YEAR

Cash Flows From Operating Activities		
Net Income		$259,996
Changes in Operating Cycle Assets and Liabilities:		
Accounts Receivable Increase	($96,404)	
Inventory Increase	($150,481)	
Prepaid Expenses Increase	($24,341)	
Accounts Payable Increase	$ 58,318	
Accrued Expenses Increase	$ 40,283	
Income Tax Payable Increase	$ 1,720	($170,905)
Operating Cash Flow, Before Depreciation		$ 89,091
Depreciation Expense		$112,792
Cash Flow From Profit-Making Operations		$201,883
Cash Flows From Investing Activities		
Purchases of Property, Plant & Equipment		($389,400)
Cash Flows From Financing Activities		
Net Increase in Short-Term Debt	$ 50,000	
Long-Term Borrowings	$ 75,000	
Capital Stock Issue	$100,000	
Cash Dividends To Stockholders	($93,750)	$131,250
Increase (Decrease) In Cash During Year		($56,267)

15

OTHER CASH FLOWS—FINANCING AND INVESTING ACTIVITIES

Internal Versus External Cash Sources:
Uses of Cash Flow

Profit is a vital source of capital to every business. Profit is the one *internal* source of capital—the money generated by the business itself without having to go outside the company to external sources of capital. The preceding chapter explains that the cash flow from the profit earned by the company during its most recent year was $201,883. This amount is less than its profit for the year, but nevertheless provided over $200,000 of available capital to the business.

Logical questions at this point are: Was this all the capital that was needed by the business, or did it need more capital? What did the company do with the $200,000-plus capital generated by its profitable operations? The remainder of the Cash Flow Statement provides the answers to these fundamentally important questions.

First of all, the company spent $389,400 for long-term operating assets; to replace those assets that reached the end of their useful lives to the business and were disposed of during the year, or to modernize certain operations and improve productivity, or for additional assets to expand its operating capacity. *Capital expenditures* is the general term for these investments (and reinvestments) in long-term operating assets.

The term "capital" has a double meaning here. It distinguishes these investments from other expenditures for operations, inventory, and prepaid items that are charged to expense immediately or fairly soon after the expenditures are made. In this sense, capital means *long-term*. Secondly, capital means just what it says—it takes capital to make these expenditures, or investments in the future. Notice that this section of the Cash Flow Statement is headed "Cash Flows From Investing Activities."

The company's capital expenditures are much more than its cash flow from profit during the year; to be more precise, $187,517 more [$389,400 capital expenditures less $201,883 cash flow from profit = $187,517]. If you were the president of the company, where would you have gotten this $187,517 of additional capital? One purpose of the third section of the Cash Flow Statement headed "Cash Flows From Financing Activities" is to answer this question.

You started the year with a Cash balance of $312,930 (see Exhibit D—Chapter 15). You could have dipped into your bank account for the $187,517, but this would have reduced your working cash balance to a fairly low ending balance.

Furthermore, assume you wanted to pay cash dividends from profit for the year. This would not have been possible if you had used your cash for capital expenditures.

So what did you do? Or, rather, what did the company do? The company increased its short-term debt by $50,000 and also borrowed an additional $75,000 from long-term debt sources. These two sources provided $125,000 of capital from interest-bearing notes payable. Also, the company asked its stockholders to put up $100,000 additional capital and issued capital stock shares for this money. Combined, debt and equity provided $225,000 capital to the company, which was more than the $187,517 needed for capital expenditures over and above cash flow from profit.

The company also paid $93,750 total cash dividends to its stockholders during the year. (We can't tell from the financial statements shown here whether dividends were paid quarterly, or just once at year-end; actual financial reports make this clear.) Cash dividends are reported in the Cash Flow Statement as a "financing activity," though personally I would have no objection to showing cash dividends as a direct deduction under cash flow from profit.

Frankly, I think reporting standards were designed to allow companies to put cash dividends down below in the Cash Flow Statement, to avoid drawing attention to the question of how much—if any—cash dividends should be paid from cash flow from profit. I suspect that most directors of publicly owned corporations would prefer not to have to defend their cash dividend decisions; it may help to avoid such questions by not putting cash dividends directly under the cash flow from profit line in the Cash Flow Statement.

Cash decreased $56,267 during the year, which is the "bottom-line" of the Cash Flow Statement. Is this good or bad? In the minds of many, a cash decrease is bad. But not so fast. The real question concerns how much cash balance a business needs. At the end of this year the company has $256,663 cash on hand, which is $56,267 less than last year (as we know from the Cash Flow Statement). Is its ending cash balance too small, too big, or about right?

There are no easy answers to this question. The $256,663 cash balance is equal to 2.2 weeks of annual sales revenue. By most standards and rules of thumb, this is a little thin; the company is cutting it a little close. Another rule of thumb is the current ratio, which is discussed in Chapter 23. We'll see there that this ratio is adequate though not robust. The company is not saddled with an inordinate amount of debt. Its stockholders' equity is more than its liabilities at the end of this year ($1,899,230 total stockholders' equity compared with $1,565,767 total liabilities).

To a large extent, it depends on how much cushion you think a business needs as a safety reserve to protect against the worst-case scenario. What if the economy took a nose dive, or if this company had a serious fall-off in sales? What if some of its accounts receivable were not collected on time? What if the company were not able to sell its inventory soon enough to start the cash flow cycle in motion? What if it ran out of cash to pay its liabilities on time? You can see why there are no easy questions to the "right" cash balance question.

In conclusion, the Cash Flow Statement deserves as much attention and scrutiny as the Income Statement and Balance Sheet. Though not too likely, a company making profit could be headed for liquidity and solvency problems, or even bankruptcy in an extreme case. Profit does not guarantee solvency. The Cash Flow Statement should be read carefully to see if there are danger signs that need attention.

16

GROWTH, DECLINE, AND CASH FLOW

The No-Growth, Steady-State Case: A Very Interesting Reference Point

A very useful baseline of reference for understanding the cash flow effects of profit is, ironically, the no-growth and no-decline, or steady-state situation. Exhibit G on the following page shows the company's financial statements for next year in exactly the same format as before, based on assumptions that sales revenue and all expenses, as well as all the basic operating ratios, are exactly the same as before. The year just ended is called *this year* in the exhibit, and the following year is called *next year*.

In essence, we're assuming no inflation, and no changes in the volume of goods sold or the "quantities" of all expenses (e.g., the number of hours worked by employees, the number of kilowatts of electricity used, and so on). Of course, this steady-state scenario with no inflation is not very realistic. Before moving on to look at the growth and decline scenarios, the steady-state case reveals several important points about cash flow from profit and the financial condition of a business.

In Exhibit G, the Income Statement for next year is an exact duplicate of this year. The Balance Sheet at the end of next year is mostly the same as at the end of this year, with a few important changes to be discussed. But notice that the Cash Flow Statement is very different!

Cash flow from profit next year is $372,788 compared with only $201,883 this year. The reason for this rather large difference, even though sales revenue and expenses are the same both years, is that none of the company's operating assets and liabilities, except for long-term operating assets, change during the next year. The ending balances are all equal to the beginning balances. Because of the opposite effects of ending and beginning balances, there is a break-even (or zero) effect on cash flow, as you can see in the Cash Flow Statement in Exhibit G.

In the no-growth situation a company does not have to increase its Accounts Receivable, Inventory, or Prepaid Expenses. In rough terms, the beginning balances are converted into cash during the year and this cash provides the ending balances, which are the same amounts.

Also, in the no-growth situation a company does not increase its Accounts Payable, Accrued Expenses, or Income Tax Payable. In rough terms, the beginning balances are paid during the year but the ending balances are not paid during the year. The beginning and ending balances are the same amounts; so, the "payoff" of the beginning balances is offset

EXHIBIT G - NO-GROWTH, STEADY-STATE EXAMPLE

INCOME STATEMENT FOR YEAR

Sales Revenue	$6,019,040
Cost of Goods Sold Expense	$3,912,376
Gross Margin	$2,106,664
Operating Expenses	$1,523,288
Operating Earnings Before Depreciation	$ 583,376
Depreciation Expense	$ 112,792
Operating Earnings	$ 470,584
Interest Expense	$ 76,650
Earnings Before Income Tax	$ 393,934
Income Tax Expense	$ 133,938
Net Income	$ 259,996

BALANCE SHEET AT END OF

Assets	Next Year	This Year
Cash	$ 422,909	$ 256,663
Accounts Receivable	$ 578,754	$ 578,754
Inventory	$ 978,094	$ 978,094
Prepaid Expenses	$ 117,176	$ 117,176
Total Current Assets	$2,096,933	$1,930,687
Property, Plant & Equipment	$2,099,242	$1,986,450
Accumulated Depreciation	($ 564,932)	($452,140)
Total Assets	$3,631,243	$3,464,997

Liabilities & Owners' Equity	Next Year	This Year
Accounts Payable:		
Inventory	$ 300,952	$ 300,952
Operating Expenses	$ 87,882	$ 87,882
Total	$ 388,834	$ 388,834
Accrued Expenses:		
Operations	$ 175,764	$ 175,764
Interest	$ 12,775	$ 12,775
Total	$ 188,539	$ 188,539
Income Tax Payable	$ 13,394	$ 13,394
Short-Term Notes Payable	$ 425,000	$ 425,000
Total Current Liabilities	$1,015,767	$1,015,767
Long-Term Notes Payable	$ 550,000	$ 550,000
Owners' Equity:		
Capital Stock	$ 725,000	$ 725,000
Retained Earnings	$1,340,476	$1,174,230
Total	$2,065,476	$1,899,230
Total Liabilities & Owners' Equity	$3,631,243	$3,464,997

CASH FLOW STATEMENT FOR NEXT YEAR

Cash Flows From Operating Activities

Net Income		$259,996
Changes in Operating Cycle Assets and Liabilities:		
Accounts Receivable Increase	$0	
Inventory Increase	$0	
Prepaid Expenses Increase	$0	
Accounts Payable Increase	$0	
Accrued Expenses Increase	$0	
Income Tax Payable Increase	$0	$0
Operating Cash Flow, Before Depreciation		$259,996
Depreciation Expense		$112,792
Cash Flow From Profit-Making Operations		$372,788

Cash Flows From Investing Activities

Purchases of Property, Plant & Equipment		($112,792)

Cash Flows From Financing Activities

Net Increase in Short-Term Debt	$0	
Long-Term Borrowings	$0	
Capital Stock Issue	$0	
Cash Dividends To Stockholders	($93,750)	($93,750)
Increase (Decrease) In Cash During Year		$1,666,246

Please Note

with an equal amount of "borrowing" in the form of the ending balances.

One other operating asset is affected in recording expenses. The long-lived operating assets decrease $112,792 next year because of the depreciation expense charged to the year (see Exhibit G). Recording depreciation expense does not decrease cash, as already explained in Chapter 14. Indeed, depreciation is the only positive cash flow factor in the Cash Flow Statement.

The company "sells off" $112,792 of its long-term assets to its customers, as it were. In other words, sales prices are set high enough to recover $112,792 of the capital originally invested in its long-term operating assets. In this sense, part of total sales revenue reimburses the business for the use of these assets in the operations of the company. There is a $112,792 "conversion" out of long-term operating assets into cash during the year. Depreciation can be quite properly thought of in this manner.

So, depreciation adds to cash flow for the year. Or, does it really? Since we are looking at a steady-state situation we should assume that the company keeps its long-term operating assets at the same level of capacity. Machines, equipment, and so on have to be replaced to maintain the capacity and services provided by the assets. Thus, the company makes capital expenditures equal exactly to the depreciation expense for the year. (Remember, we are assuming no inflation in this example.) In short, capital expenditures offset the depreciation, so from the cash flow point of view there is no increase.

The company earns $259,996 next year—without any increases in its current assets and current liabilities that are affected by its sales revenue and expenses. All the net income is available in cash—which you can see with the string of zeros in the Cash Flow Statement for the operating assets and liabilities. In summary, cash flow from profit before depreciation equals exactly net income for the year. The accrual basis and cash flow basis of profit accounting yield the same amount in this steady-state situation.

What did the company do with the $259,996 cash flow provided by net income? The business paid $93,750 cash dividends. There are no stock issues and no increases in debt during the year, which are reasonable assumptions in this steady-state situation. So, the bottom line is that Cash increases $166,246 next year.

Also, please note that Retained Earnings increases by the net income less the cash dividends. What else? You might also note that the Accumulated Depreciation contra account has one more year of depreciation in it at the end of next year.*

*We could have assumed that some long-term depreciable assets were disposed of during the year, which would have removed the cost of the assets from the Property, Plant & Equipment account and the total depreciation recorded over the years on the assets from the Accumulated Depreciation account. To keep the example reasonably simple to follow this aspect is avoided.

Growth and Cash Flow

Growth is the central strategy of most, if not the large majority, of businesses. The purpose of growth, of course, is to increase profit and shareholders' wealth—although without good management, expenses may grow faster than sales revenue and profit may actually decrease. In tough times just holding its own may be the best a business can do. And don't forget that virtually every business faces the threat of decline that leads to profit shrinkage or loss, and even bankruptcy. The remainder of this chapter examines the *cash flow* impacts of growth and decline.

Making profit in the steady-state scenario presented at the start of the chapter—i.e., flat sales revenue and profit performance year to year—is like "milking a cash cow." The profit cow delivers operating cash flow equal to bottom-line profit plus depreciation—please refer to Exhibit G. Even in this situation, however, not all of the cash flow from profit may be *free* cash, i.e., available for whatever alternatives the company may have in mind. To maintain operating capacity the business has to replace its long-term assets that reach the end of their useful economic lives during the year. Furthermore, the replacement costs of these long-term operating assets may be considerably higher than their original cost some years ago.

In the steady-state example shown in Exhibit G, replacement cost is set equal to original cost depreciation. As you can see, during the year capital expenditures for property, plant, and equipment are $112,792 which equals exactly the depreciation recorded for the year. In other words, it is assumed that there had been no inflation over the years. But this is rather unrealistic. For most businesses, annual depreciation recovery is substantially less than the replacement cost of new long-term operating assets. So depreciation recovery is not enough; some of the company's operating cash flow must be earmarked for replacement cost inflation.

With this in mind, let's move on to the growth situation. We should distinguish between *inflation* growth and *real* growth. Inflation growth means that sales prices, costs, and expenses go up with no increase in sales volume, or actual number of units sold. In this situation a business does not have to expand its operating capacity because only dollar values increase, not the real number of units sold.

Real growth means an increase in the number of units sold which brings with it an increase in the level of organizational activity that supports sales. A business may have enough unused operating capacity or organizational slack that it could take on a modest amount of real growth without having to expand its long-term operating assets or hire more employees. But sooner or later the business will hit the limit of its operating capacity. To continue to grow, the company will have to make capital expenditures for expansion, in addition to the capital expenditures needed to replace those assets that reach the end of their useful lives. The key question is: Will higher profit generate cash flow to help provide growth capital? Probably not! At least not in the short run. Growth should be good for profit next year, but is almost always bad for cash flow next year.

Let's run through a growth case scenario for next year, in place of the steady-state, no-growth example illustrated earlier in the chapter. The main focus is on operating cash flow before depreciation, which is reported in the Cash Flow Statement. Several assumptions have to be made. If sales revenue were to increase, say 20%, this does not mean that bottom-line profit would automatically increase 20%—life is not so simple. At this point do not be too concerned about the company's profit performance next year; profit increases more than 20%, which is a reasonable scenario.

All key operating ratios explained in the previous chapters remain the same in this growth example. For instance, the ending Accounts Receivable balance equals 5 weeks of annual sales revenue, the inventory holding period is 13 weeks, and so on. We assume that company can take on 20% sales revenue growth without expanding its operating capacity. In other words, the company has enough idle capacity or slack that allows it to operate at the higher sales volume level *without* making capital expenditures for expansion. In the example the company neither borrows any new money nor issues any cap-ital stock shares. In short, the company does not tap any *external* sources of capital during the year. Cash flow from profit-making operations is its *only* source of capital.

Exhibit H presents the 20% growth case example, keeping in mind the assumptions just mentioned. Profit moves up nicely, from $259,996 in the no-growth case to $393,859—an increase of $133,863! But notice what happens to operating cash flow before depreciation. Instead of increasing $133,863 with profit, cash flow *decreases* $89,039 compared with the no-growth situation. (Operating cash flow is $259,996 in the no-growth case but only $170,957 in the growth case, which is a $89,039 decrease—see Exhibits H and G.) In summary, growth helps profit but hurts cash flow.

You can see why in Exhibit H. The three short-term operating assets (Accounts Receivable, Inventory, and Prepaid Expenses) increase, and the three short-term operating liabilities (Accounts Payable, Accrued Expenses, and Income Tax Payable) also increase. The net effect is a $222,902 cash flow "take away" from profit. Profit is earned but cash flow is not realized to this extent.* Growth will do this. Growth brings with it an increase in the net short-term operating capital needed by the business, which decreases the cash flow from profit.

To avoid or minimize the negative impacts of growth on cash flow from profit, a business could attempt to improve its operating ratios. This could be done by reducing its average collection period of accounts receivable, or its average inven-

---

* You might notice that the $222,902 increase in the net short-term operating capital caused by growth is $89,039 more than the $133,863 profit increase. This is why cash flow from profit decreases $89,039, compared with the no-growth, steady-state case.

EXHIBIT H - GROWTH EXAMPLE

INCOME STATEMENT FOR YEAR

Sales Revenue	$7,222,848
Cost of Goods Sold Expense	$4,694,851
Gross Margin	$2,527,997
Operating Expenses	$1,736,548
Operating Earnings Before Depreciation	$ 791,448
Depreciation Expense	$ 112,792
Operating Earnings	$ 678,656
Interest Expense	$ 81,900
Earnings Before Income Tax	$ 596,756
Income Tax Expense	$ 202,897
Net Income	$ 393,859

BALANCE SHEET AT END OF

Assets	This Year	Last Year
Cash	$ 333,870	$ 256,663
Accounts Receivable	$ 694,505	$ 578,754
Inventory	$1,173,713	$ 978,094
Prepaid Expenses	$ 133,581	$ 117,176
Total Current Assets	$2,335,668	$1,930,687
Property, Plant & Equipment	$2,099,242	$1,986,450
Accumulated Depreciation	($ 564,932)	($452,140)
Total Assets	$3,869,978	$3,464,997

Liabilities & Owners' Equity	This Year	Last Year
Accounts Payable:		
Inventory	$ 361,142	$ 300,952
Operating Expenses	$ 100,185	$ 87,882
Total	$ 461,328	$ 388,834
Accrued Expenses:		
Operations	$ 200,371	$ 175,764
Interest	$ 13,650	$ 12,775
Total	$ 214,021	$ 188,539
Income Tax Payable	$ 20,290	$ 13,394
Short-Term Notes Payable	$ 425,000	$ 425,000
Total Current Liabilities	$1,120,639	$1,015,767
Long-Term Notes Payable	$ 550,000	$ 550,000
Owners' Equity:		
Capital Stock	$ 725,000	$ 725,000
Retained Earnings	$1,474,339	$1,174,230
Total	$2,199,339	$1,899,230
Total Liabilities & Owners' Equity	$3,869,978	$3,464,997

CASH FLOW STATEMENT FOR NEXT YEAR

Cash Flows From Operating Activities		
Net Income		$398,017
Changes in Operating Cycle Assets and Liabilities:		
Accounts Receivable Increase	($115,751)	
Inventory Increase	($195,619)	
Prepaid Expenses Increase	($ 16,405)	
Accounts Payable Increase	$ 72,494	
Accrued Expenses Increase	$ 25,482	
Income Tax Payable Increase	$ 6,896	($222,902)
Operating Cash Flow, Before Depreciation		$170,957
Depreciation Expense		$112,792
Cash Flow From Profit-Making Operations		$283,749
Cash Flows From Investing Activities		
Purchases of Property, Plant & Equipment		($112,792)
Cash Flows From Financing Activities		
Net Increase in Short-Term Debt	$0	
Long-Term Borrowings	$0	
Capital Stock Issue	$0	
Cash Dividends To Stockholders	($93,750)	($93,750)
Increase (Decrease) In Cash During Year		$ 77,207

—Please Note—

Growth, decline, and cash flow 83

tory holding period, or stretching out its average accounts payable payment period, and so on. However, during growth periods improving operating ratios is not too practical. If anything, the operating ratios may move the wrong way. The company may offer its customers more liberal credit terms to stimulate sales, which would extend the average accounts receivable collection period. Or, the business may increase the size and mix of its inventory to improve delivery times to customers to provide better selection.

To sum up, cash flow from profit cannot carry the whole load and provide *all* the capital needed to finance growth. What are the alternatives? Possibly the business could have a sufficiently large cash balance on hand, or the company could conserve cash by not paying cash dividends. More often than not, however, the business will have to go to external debt and/or equity sources of capital to finance growth.

Decline and Cash Flow

The old saying, "what goes up can come down," certainly applies to sales revenue. Few businesses can keep growing forever, although there are examples of long-run sustained growth, such as Wal-Mart. Some industries are cyclical by nature; sales revenue goes up and down like a roller coaster over the cycle. Unless you have been lost in the Amazon for some time, you are undoubtedly aware that the late 1980s and early 1990s were not kind and gentle to many businesses. Even some very well-known and respected names suffered reverses of fortune and steep declines. Quite clearly the past does not always predict the future.

Profit performance almost always suffers in a decline. For an illustrative example here we assume a 20% sales revenue decline, which is a minor disaster though not a catastrophe. For the sake of the example we assume that the company's managers take timely and tough measures to control expenses such that the company breaks even and avoids slipping into the loss column.* Bottom-line profit is zero in this example.

* You might think that the company could simply reduce all its expenses by 20% such that profit would decrease only 20% instead of dropping to zero (which is a 100% decrease). However, it is unlikely that all expenses could be reduced 20%.

This assumption provides a very useful point of reference for examining what happens to cash flow from profit.

Given the steep decline in sales, the company does not replace any of its long-term operating assets. Furthermore, no new money is borrowed and no new capital stock shares are issued.

Exhibit I presents the 20% decline scenario. In the steady-state example presented earlier in the chapter the company earns profit; with the decline in sales all the profit disappears. Would operating cash flow also disappear? As a matter of fact, it would not; operating cash flow before depreciation is a healthy $235,077 and the business also realizes $112,792 cash flow from depreciation recovery, for total operating cash flow of $347,869.

Cash flow is good even though profit performance is nil. Why? The basic reasons are the same as in the growth case except that everything works in reverse. The key point concerns *operating ratios*. As in the growth case all the company's operating ratios are kept the same. The average accounts receivable collection period is 5 weeks, the average inventory holding period is 13 weeks, and so on. Therefore, the three short-term operating assets decline with the decline in sales

EXHIBIT I - DECLINE EXAMPLE

BALANCE SHEET AT END OF

INCOME STATEMENT FOR NEXT YEAR

Sales Revenue	$4,815,232
Cost of Goods Sold Expense	$3,129,901
Gross Margin	$1,685,331
Operating Expenses	$1,496,939
Operating Earnings Before Depreciation	$ 188,392
Depreciation Expense	$ 112,792
Operating Earnings	$ 75,600
Interest Expense	$ 75,600
Earnings Before Income Tax	$ 0
Income Tax Expense	$ 0
Net Income	$ 0

Assets	Next Year	This Year
Cash	$ 510,782	$ 256,663
Accounts Receivable	$ 463,003	$ 578,754
Inventory	$ 782,475	$ 978,094
Prepaid Expenses	$ 115,149	$ 117,176
Total Current Assets	$1,871,409	$1,930,687
Property, Plant & Equipment	$1,986,450	$1,986,450
Accumulated Depreciation	($564,932)	($452,140)
Total Assets	$3,292,927	$3,464,997

Liabilities & Owners' Equity	Nexy Year	This Year
Accounts Payable:		
Inventory	$ 240,762	$ 300,952
Operating Expenses	$ 86,362	$ 87,882
Total	$ 327,123	$ 388,834
Accrued Expenses:		
Operations	$ 172,724	$ 175,764
Interest	$ 12,600	$ 12,775
Total	$ 185,324	$ 188,539
Income Tax Payable	$ 0	$ 13,394
Short-Term Notes Payable	$ 425,000	$ 425,000
Total Current Liabilities	$ 937,447	$1,015,767
Long-Term Notes Payable	$ 550,000	$ 550,000
Owners' Equity:		
Capital Stock	$ 725,000	$ 725,000
Retained Earnings	$1,080,480	$1,174,230
Total	$1,805,480	$1,899,230
Total Liabilities & Owners' Equity	$3,292,927	$3,464,997

CASH FLOW STATEMENT FOR NEXT YEAR

Cash Flows From Operating Activities

Net Income		$0
Changes in Operating Cycle Assets and Liabilities:		
Accounts Receivable Decrease	$115,751	
Inventory Decrease	$195,619	
Prepaid Expenses Decrease	$ 2,027	
Accounts Payable Decrease	($61,711)	
Accrued Expenses Decrease	($3,215)	
Income Tax Payable Decrease	($13,394)	$235,077
Operating Cash Flow, Before Depreciation		$235,077
Depreciation Expense		$112,792
Cash Flow From Profit-Making Operations		$347,869

Cash Flows From Investing Activities

Purchases of Property, Plant & Equipment	$0

Cash Flows From Financing Activities

Short-Term Debt	$0	
Long-Term Borrowing	$0	
Capital Stock Issue	$0	
Cash Dividends To Stockholders	($93,750)	($93,750)
Increase (Decrease) In Cash During Year		$254,119

Please Note

Growth, decline, and cash flow

revenue and expenses. Also, the three short-term operating liabilities decline. (Notice that since the company breaks even it has no taxable income and no income tax expense for the year; at the end of the year Income Tax Payable is down to zero.)

To sum up, there is a $235,077 "liquidation" in the net short-term operating capital needed by the business. In other words, there is a downsizing in the net amount of capital invested in the three short-term operating assets, which is partially offset with the pay-down on the three short-term operating liabilities. In short, at the lower level of sales and expense activity the company needs less capital to operate and total cash flow from operations is $347,869. What should the company do with this cash flow?

In Exhibit I the company is shown paying $93,750 cash dividends, even though profit for the year is zero. This is not illegal, although the board of directors may decide not to declare any cash dividends in a year of no profit. Cash dividends can be paid out of prior years' profits. Indeed, the large balance in Retained Earnings means that cash dividends over the years have been much lower than profit over the years.

The broader issues concern the future of the business and developing a survival and rebound strategy for the company. Notice that the cash balance at the end of the year is $510,782. This is not excessively large, but then again you could argue that the company does not need this much operating cash balance (unless the company predicts a quick turnaround the following year).

Downsizing a business by disposing of or mothballing some of its long-term operating assets and laying off employees is very painful for everyone, to say the least. Many companies delay making such radical decisions. For one thing, downsizing means top management is giving up on the future and can't find alternatives to maintain the size of the firm or to grow. But isn't this exactly the very core function of top management—to know how to take the business forward into the future?

In the worst-case scenario a business can't control its decline. It cannot or will not reduce its expenses commensurate with the decline in its sales revenue. Furthermore, the business may not collect its receivables in a timely manner and may not reduce its inventory to keep up (or "keep down") with the decline in sales revenue. So, cash flow suffers.

Often a business in this situation ends up writing off receivables it can't collect and inventory it can't sell. Cash flow may be so bad that the business soon runs out of cash and defaults on its debt payment schedules. Soon the company may be at the mercy of its creditors, or the business may file for bankruptcy protection from its creditors. Cash flow analysis, as discussed in this chapter, is absolutely essential in a bankruptcy workout situation.

17

FOOTNOTES—THE FINE PRINT IN FINANCIAL REPORTS

Pick up any annual financial report and you'll see the Balance Sheet, Income Statement, and Cash Flow Statement. Also you'll find two pages or more of footnotes. Footnotes provide the "fine print" that goes along with the three principal financial statements.

Top-level managers should never forget that they are responsible for the financial statements and the accompanying footnotes. The footnotes are an integral, inseparable part of the financial report. In fact, financial reports state this on the bottom of each page of the financial statements, usually somewhat as follows:

> The accompanying footnotes to the financial statements are an integral part of these statements.

The auditor's report (see the next chapter) covers the footnotes as well as the financial statements. In short, footnotes are necessary for *adequate disclosure* in financial reports.

Two Basic Types of Footnotes

Basically, there are two kinds of footnotes. First, the major *accounting policies* of the business have to be identified and briefly explained. The company's cost of goods sold expense method has to be identified (see Chapter 21 for discussion of these methods). And its depreciation method has to be identified (see Chapter 22). In short, if more than one generally accepted accounting method is allowed, the company's choice of method has to be disclosed. (Chapter 19 discusses the manager's responsibility for these key accounting choices.)

In addition to the key accounting choices of the business, other accounting premises and methods used to prepare the financial statements may be disclosed in footnotes. For example, many larger businesses consist of a family of corporations under the control of one parent corporation. Separate corporations are consolidated into one set of financial statements. However, affiliated companies in which the company has an equity interest but *not a controlling* interest are *not* consolidated.

The second type of footnotes provide *additional disclosure* that cannot be placed in the main body of the financial statements. For example, the maturity dates, interest rates, collateral or other security provisions, and other details of the long-term debt of a business are presented in a footnote; annual rentals required under operating leases are given; details regarding any stock option or employee stock ownership plans are spelled out; and the status of major lawsuits and other legal actions against the company are discussed.

Details about its employees' retirement and pension plans are also disclosed. Pension plan disclosure, in fact, is very complex but very important. The list of possible footnotes is a long one. In summary, many Balance Sheet accounts need additional footnote disclosure.

The Manager's Decision Regarding Footnotes

Managers have to rely on the experts—their chief financial officer or the CPA auditor—to go through the checklist of footnotes that may be required. Once each required footnote has been identified, the manager should realize that there is still an important decision to make regarding each footnote. There is still a fair amount of management discretion or judgment required regarding just how frank to be and how much detail to reveal in the footnote.

Clearly the manager should not divulge information that would cause a loss of or decline in any competitive advantage the business now enjoys. Managers don't have to help their competitors—the idea is to help the debtholders and stockholders of the business, to report to them information they are entitled to. But just how much information do the debtholders and stockholders need or are they legally entitled to? This question is very difficult to answer. Beyond certain minimum basics and details, the extent of "required" or "fair" disclosure in footnotes is *not* all that clear.

Too little disclosure, such as withholding information about a major lawsuit against the business, for instance, would be misleading and the top managers are legally liable for this lack of disclosure. Beyond this "legal minimum," which will be insisted on by the CPA auditors, rules and guidelines are vague and murky. The manager has a fairly broad freedom of choice in how far to go and how frank to be.

Incomprehensible Footnotes:
A Serious Problem to Creditors and Investors

One last point concerns the readability of footnotes. As an author I may be overly sensitive to this, but I think not. Footnote writing sometimes is so poor that you have to suspect that the writing is deliberately obscure. The rules require footnotes, but the rules do not require that the footnotes be clear and concise so the average financial report reader can understand them.

Frequently the sentence structure of footnotes seems intentionally legalistic and awkward. Terminology is very technical. Poor writing seems more prevalent in footnotes on sensitive matters, such as lawsuits lost or still in progress or ventures the business has abandoned with heavy losses. A lack of candor in many footnotes is obvious.

Creditors and stockholders cannot expect managers to expose all the dirty wash of the business in footnotes, or to confess all their bad decisions. But more clarity and frankness certainly would help and would not damage the business.

The stockholders can ask questions at their annual meetings with management and the board of directors. However, managers can be just as evasive in their answers as in the footnotes.

In short, creditors and investors frequently are stymied by poorly written footnotes. You really have only one choice, and that's to plow slowly through the troublesome footnotes, more than once if necessary. Usually you can tell if the footnote is important enough to deserve this extra effort.

18

THE COST OF CREDIBILITY—
AUDITS BY CPAs

Why Audits?

Suppose you have invested a lot of money in a business but are not involved in managing the company. You're an "absentee owner." As one of the owners you receive the company's financial reports. The previous chapters have explained how to read and understand the reports. But how do you know that the financial reports are correct? Can you rely on the reports?

Or, suppose you are a bank loan officer and a business presents its financial report as part of the loan application package. Are the financial statements correct? How do you know?

Or, consider a corporation whose stock shares are traded on the New York Stock Exchange. The market value of the shares depends on the earnings record and other information presented in its financial reports. How do the stockholders know that the corporation's financial reports are correct?

The answer to this basic question is to have financial reports audited by independent *certified public accountants.*

Based on the audit, the CPA expresses an opinion on the financial report—an opinion that the business has followed generally acceptable accounting and disclosure standards in preparing its financial report. This opinion provides assurance that the financial report can be relied on by creditors and investors. In short, audits increase the credibility of financial reports.

Who's a certified public accountant? What is an audit of a company's financial statements? Are audits by CPAs required? Even if not required, should a business have its financial statements audited by an independent CPA? What are the limits of audits by CPAs? Do audits detect management fraud? Will they catch all errors? Should a business use an outside CPA to help prepare its financial statements but *not* have its statements audited?

These are the main questions addressed in this chapter.

Certified versus
Noncertified Public Accountants

A person needs to do three things to become a *certified* public accountant (CPA). He or she must earn a college degree with a fairly heavy major (emphasis) in accounting courses. By the turn of the century many states will require a five-year college program to satisfy the education requirement. Then the person must pass the national uniform CPA exam. Third, a person needs practical, on-the-job experience working for a CPA firm (in most states).

After all three basic requirements are completed—education, the exam, and experience—the person receives the license by his or her state of residence to practice as a CPA. No one else may hold himself or herself out as a CPA. Most states require continuing education requirements to be satisfied to renew the CPA license. The State Boards of Accountancy in all states maintain a directory of those licensed to practice as a CPA in that state.

Those who have not met all the requirements can offer accounting and income tax services to the public, although they seldom do audits. They are called public accountants, or registered accountants. The use of this title and the regulation of non-CPAs vary from state to state. The main reason public accountants are not CPAs is that they have not passed the CPA exam, which is very rigorous and requires thorough preparation to pass.

Are Audits by CPAs Required?

Publicly owned corporations whose debt and/or stock securities are traded on a stock exchange or over-the-counter are required by federal securities laws to have their annual financial reports audited by an independent CPA firm. These include about 10,000 corporations in the United States today.

Beyond this group it is more difficult to generalize about which businesses are legally required to have their financial reports audited by CPAs, either annually or on certain occasions. There may be a legal need for an audit when raising capital through issuing debt or equity securities, even if the securities do not come under federal law. Lawyers should be consulted regarding state corporation and securities laws. Also, as a condition of borrowing money or issuing stock, a business can agree to have its annual financial reports audited.

But there are thousands and thousands of businesses that are not legally required to have their financial statements audited by CPAs. Neither federal nor state laws require the audits, and the businesses have not bound themselves by contract to have audits.

Even if Not Required, Should a Business Have Its Financial Report Audited by an Independent CPA?

Basically, audits by independent CPAs add *credibility* to the financial statements of a business. Audited financial statements have a higher credibility index than unaudited ones.

There are two reasons why unaudited financial statements of a business can be wrong and seriously misleading:

1. *Honest mistakes* resulting from an inadequate accounting system or an inadequate understanding of accounting principles and financial reporting standards.

2. *Deliberate dishonesty* by a business manager who distorts the amounts reported in the financial statements or withholds important information.

Audits guard against both of these causes of misleading financial statements. Auditors are expert accounting system "detectives," and they thoroughly understand accounting principles and reporting standards. And, being independent of the business, the CPA auditor will not tolerate management dishonesty in the financial statements.

Be warned that the cost of an audit is high. The business manager cannot really bargain over how much auditing will be done. An audit is an audit. The CPA is bound by generally accepted auditing standards (GAAS), which are the authoritative rules in doing audits. There is no such thing as a "bargain basement" audit, or a "quick and dirty, once over lightly" audit. Violations of GAAS can result in legal suits against the CPA or may damage the CPA's professional reputation.

An audit requires a lot of work before the auditor can express an opinion on the financial statements (including footnotes). This results in the relatively high cost of an audit. The manager has to ask whether the gain in credibility is worth the cost of an audit.

A bank may insist on regular audits as a condition of making loans to a business. Or, those stockholders not directly involved in the day-to-day management of the business may insist on annual audits to protect their investment in the business. In these cases the audit is a cost of using "outside" capital. But in many situations the outside sources of capital do not insist on audits. In these cases should a business have an audit?

Perhaps one or more of its employees are stealing money or other assets, accepting kickbacks, or manipulating sales prices for relatives or friends. The record of employee theft and dishonesty is not a good one, unfortunately. An audit may uncover employee theft and dishonesty, or deter potential theft and dishonesty. But this is *not* the main purpose of an audit of financial reports.

A business should not have an audit if, in fact, it wants a security check. The business should ask the CPA to come in and closely study and evaluate its internal controls to deter and detect employee theft and dishonesty. This sort of investigation may be very useful, but it is *not* an audit of the financial report, which is for a different purpose.

What Are Audits? What's a "Clean" Opinion?

First, let's be very clear on one point. We're talking about audits of financial reports by CPAs. There are many other types of audits, such as audits by the Internal Revenue Service of taxpayer returns, audits of federally supported programs by the General Accounting Office, in-house audits by the internal auditors of an organization, and so on. The following discussion concerns audits of financial reports by CPAs for the purpose of the CPA expressing an opinion on the report.

Financial report users are not too concerned about how an audit is done, nor should they be. The bottom line to them is the opinion of the CPA. They should read the opinion carefully, although there is some evidence that most don't. Evidently, many users simply assume that having the financial report audited is, itself, an adequate check, or safeguard. They may assume that the CPA would not be associated with any financial report that is misleading or incorrect.

You've heard of "guilt by association," haven't you? Well, you could say that in the case of audits by CPAs there's a kind of reverse approach. Many, perhaps most, users of financial reports assume "innocence by association"—if the CPA gives an opinion and thereby is associated with the financial report, then the report must be OK, or at least not seriously misleading. Doesn't the CPA's opinion constitute a "stamp of approval"? Not necessarily!

The CPA auditing profession has gone to great lengths to define the limits of the audit opinion and to differentiate between several types of audit opinions.

The best audit opinion is called an *unqualified* opinion, or more popularly a "clean" opinion. Basically, this opinion states that the CPA has no material disagreements with the financial report. In other words, the CPA attests that the financial report has been prepared according to generally accepted accounting and disclosure principles. (This still leaves management a wide range of choices, as the next chapter explains.)

In a clean opinion the CPA auditor says, "I don't disagree with the financial report." The CPA might have prepared the report differently; in fact, the CPA might prefer that different accounting methods had been used. All the CPA says in a clean opinion is that the accounting and disclosure presented in the financial report is acceptable.

Starting with 1988 financial reports the auditor's standard unqualified, or "clean" opinion report reads as follows:

Independent Auditor's Report

We have audited the accompanying balance sheets of X Company as of December 31, 19X2 and 19X1, and the related statements of income, retained earnings, and cash flows for the years then ended. These financial statements are the responsibility of the Company's management. Our responsibility is to express an opinion on these financial statements based on our audits.

We conducted our audits in accordance with generally accepted auditing standards. Those standards require that we plan and perform the audit to obtain reasonable assurance about whether the financial statements are free of material misstatement. An audit includes examining, on a test basis, evidence supporting the amounts and disclosures in the financial statements. An audit also includes assessing the accounting principles used and significant estimates made by management, as well as evaluating the overall financial statement presentation. We believe that our audits provide a reasonable basis for our opinion.

In our opinion, the financial statements referred to above present fairly, in all material respects, the financial position of X Company as of December 31, 19X2 and 19X1, and results of its operations and its cash flows for the years then ended in conformity with generally accepted accounting principles.

This new wording was adopted by the national professional association of CPAs, the American Institute of Certified Public Accountants (AICPA), to close the so-called "expectations gap" by users of financial reports. The AICPA was of the opinion that investors and creditors did not adequately understand the primary role of management in preparing the financial report, so this point is mentioned in the first paragraph. Also, the AICPA thought that it should be made clear that audits provide reasonable but not absolute assurance that the financial statements are free of material accounting errors and provide all significant disclosures. Last, it was thought that the users of financial statements should be told briefly what an audit involves.

Whether the new wording has in fact closed the expectations gap is a matter of opinion. I think not. The new version runs 200 words of fairly technical jargon and asks a lot of the reader. In my opinion, creditors and investors still have the same basic expectation—that they can rely on audited financial statements.

Financial statements that have been "blessed" with a clean opinion by the CPA auditor may later turn out to have been misleading, causing losses to creditors and investors. The auditor is almost always sued in these situations.

Overall, audits have an excellent track record—not very many fraudulent or materially misleading financial reports get by the CPA auditor with a clean opinion. But some do; audits are not perfect. The cost of an audit that would increase to 100% the probability of catching all material errors and all fraudulent intrigues would be prohibitive. There are occasional audit failures. The cost of eliminating all audit failures is too high a price to pay. In the grand scheme of things a few audit failures are tolerated to control the overall cost of audits.

Additional Language in Unqualified Opinions and Qualified Opinions

In some situations the CPA auditor must extend the unqualified (clean) opinion with additional explanatory comments. The standard clean opinion consists of three rather long paragraphs (see page 102). Nevertheless, a fourth paragraph is necessary: (a) if there are major uncertainties that cannot be estimated in any reasonable manner and, thus, are not yet accounted for in the financial statements; (b) the company has changed its accounting principles or methods between this and previous years; and (c) there is substantial doubt about the entity's ability to continue as a going concern. All three of these situations are very important for creditors and investors to be aware of, so the AICPA has decided that they should be mentioned in the auditor's report.

A "four paragraph" clean or unqualified audit opinion is different than a *qualified* audit opinion that is issued when the CPA takes exception to an accounting method used by the company or when the CPA finds fault with the disclosure in the financial report. The CPA is satisfied that the financial report taken as a whole is not misleading but nevertheless takes exception with one or more items in the statement because the company has departed from the established rules, i.e., generally accepted accounting principles. The Securities and Exchange Commission (SEC) generally will not accept qualified audit reports, because the company could change its accounting or disclosure to avoid the qualified opinion. For nonpublic companies, however, you'll see qualified opinions.

How serious a matter is a qualified opinion? Basically, it has a "fly in the ointment" effect. The auditor is pointing out a flaw in the financial report, but not a fatal flaw. It's a yellow flag, but not a red flag. The auditor must be satisfied that the overall fairness of the financial report is satisfactory, even though there are one or more departures from established accounting and disclosure standards. If the auditor is of the opinion that the exceptions are so serious as to make the financial report misleading, the CPA must go much further and give an *adverse* opinion. You hardly ever see an adverse opinion. No company wants to issue misleading financial reports and have the auditor say so.

Do Auditors Detect Management Fraud?
Does Business Failure Mean Audit Failure?

Let's go straight to a longtime bone of contention between CPA auditors and those who rely on audited financial reports (the users). The users, in my opinion, understand that the basic purpose of an audit is to "check over financial statements and to make sure everything is alright." I don't think users expect CPA auditors to catch minor errors and petty theft. But, users do expect CPA auditors to detect management fraud and major errors, and when auditors don't uncover such deceptions and massive mistakes, users are quick to sue on grounds of professional malpractice.

Of course, auditors don't like getting sued. Recent years have been tough ones for large national CPA firms. They have paid millions of dollars to settle many lawsuits and have seen their good names dragged through one story after another in the press. It's possible that the press coverage is more extensive than it used to be, though I don't think so. The evidence is fairly convincing that there have been more cases of management fraud during recent years.

Very few of the management frauds that have come to light during recent years were the result of audit discovery. Many of the schemes collapsed from their own weight; things got so far beyond control that the guilty parties could not keep the game going. In some cases there was a falling-out among the parties to the conspiracy. Or, a whistle-blower tipped off the authorities. In a few cases security analysts raised some hard questions that could not be answered by the business.

Why didn't audits detect the more flagrant cases of management fraud and substantial accounting mistakes that were found out eventually?

First of all, the guilty parties went to great effort and were skillful at concealing their frauds for some time. In particular, they generated counterfeit evidence to mislead the auditors. This is a key point. Auditors, in the last analysis, audit evidence, and there is not enough time to validate every important piece of evidence that auditors examine. If evidence looks credible on the surface it is generally accepted, unless other audit procedures raise doubts and questions about the evidence.

Another reason why audits fail to detect management fraud is that of small audit samples. In many areas of an audit only a relatively small number from a large population of items is examined. For instance, auditors usually do not inspect every item in inventory; they rely on test samples. The small sample approach is based on the theory of adequate internal controls that are instituted and enforced by the business to prevent errors and deliberate dishonesty. Auditors test internal controls to determine that the controls are effective. But managers know how to override internal controls and they have the authority to do so.

In summary, crooks always have the advantage over auditors. From a cost/benefit point of view, there is no way that auditors can look for every conceivable type of fraud. And auditors do not have the time to validate every piece of evidence during the course of an audit. Collusion among two or more employees, especially among top-level managers who have broad authority, is very difficult to discover by normal audit procedures.

Auditors have gone to a great deal of effort over the years to delimit their responsibility for the detection of management fraud that results in misleading financial statements. These attempts can be found in the history of the authoritative pronouncements that govern audit procedures and audit report standards, called *Statements on Auditing Standards*. These standards have not been very successful in limiting the legal liability of auditors, however.

I should mention that CPA auditors get a bum rap on one point. Many times *business* failures are confused with audit failures. Even well-managed businesses can have a quick reversal of fortunes. A clean audit opinion does not mean that the auditor is guaranteeing the future solvency and financial health of the company. Anything can happen.

As mentioned earlier, financial statement users should look for a possible fourth paragraph in the audit report. The auditor adds this paragraph if there is serious concern about the continued existence of the business entity. If the auditor does add this paragraph then "forewarned is forearmed." The user cannot come back later and complain that the business went into bankruptcy and the auditors are to blame.

Auditors cannot be held responsible for bad management and the inability of a business to work itself out of a financial distress situation. Users have the responsibility to be alert for financial problems the company may be facing. Indeed, one basic purpose of financial statements is to provide information for users to diagnose the solvency prospects of the business. However, if there is substantial doubt concerning the ability of the business to survive in the short-run, then the auditor must add the fourth paragraph in the audit report as a warning signal. If auditors fail to do this they will be held liable.

In case the above discussion sounds too negative, let me add in closing that CPA auditors make financial reports a lot better than they would be without audits. Based on my experience and discussions with other CPAs, auditors are very effective watchdogs. They persuade companies to make many improvements in their accounting methods and disclosures that would not be done without the pressure from the independent auditor. All in all, the "bang for the buck" from audits is reasonable—even though audits do not detect high-level management fraud very often.

Using a CPA to Review or Prepare Financial Statements Instead of Auditing Them

An audit may be too costly; the cost of the audit could be more than the total interest on the loan to a smaller business. Bankers and other sources of loans to business understand this. Often lenders do not insist on an audit. Yet they prefer that a CPA at least "look over" the financial reports of companies they loan money to.

A CPA can perform certain limited procedures called a *review*. A review is *far less* than a full-scale audit. But a review does provide the CPA with a basis of information about the financial report. Based on the review, the CPA can state that he or she is not aware of any modifications (changes) that are needed to make the financial statements conform with generally accepted accounting principles. This is said in the final paragraph of the CPA's report. However, the CPA (reviewer) also warns the reader earlier in the report that a review is substantially less than an audit and that, accordingly, no opinion is being expressed on the financial report.

In short, based on a review, the CPA does not give an affirmative opinion report; instead, the auditor gives a negative assurance ("no modifications are needed . . . "). This negative assurance may be enough to satisfy the lender.

When an audit or a review is done by a CPA the financial statements are prepared by the business itself. Many smaller companies, on the other hand, need the help of a CPA to prepare their financial statements in the first place. These companies don't have a professionally qualified accountant on their payroll. They use a CPA as a "part-time Controller" (chief accountant) to pull together their financial statements.

In this situation the CPA is said to *compile* the financial statements. No audit and no review is done; so, the CPA must disclaim any opinion on the financial report, and no negative assurance may be given either.

19

MANIPULATING THE NUMBERS
(OR, COOKING THE BOOKS)

The Name of the Game

Financial reports are prepared in conformity with certain established standards called *Generally Accepted Accounting Principles* (GAAP). Rarely, if ever, would you come across a financial report of a business that states GAAP have not been followed. Audits of financial reports by CPAs are precisely for the purpose of making sure that the company has complied with GAAP in preparing its financial report (see Chapter 18).

Basically, a business has to *play fair* in reporting its profit-making operations (Income Statement), its financial condition (Balance Sheet), and its cash flows (Cash Flow Statement)—as well as providing additional disclosure in footnotes. In other words, the established standards (GAAP) should be followed in measuring sales revenue and expenses to determine profit (net income) and to determine asset, liability, and owners' equity values—the "numbers."

You may be under the impression that once the facts of a company's transactions and operations have been determined there emerges one and only one set of accounting numbers. However, you should know that the same facts do *not* lead to the same numbers. Financial accounting would seem to be like measuring a person's weight, wouldn't it? But in fact, financial accounting also involves choosing the scale—one that weighs light or one that weights heavy, or possibly one that weighs in between. In short, for many financial statement numbers there's not just one rule, but two rules or even three rules. The game can be played fairly by any one of the rules. Choices must be made from among *alternative*, equally accepted accounting methods.

The conditions of each case do *not* dictate the method that has to be used. For example, in periods of rising costs, either a conservative "keep the profits down" Cost of Goods Sold Expense method may be used, or a more generous method may be used. And in periods of stable costs, either method may be selected. For another example: Regardless of whether long-lived asset replacement costs are increasing or holding level, either a rapid (accelerated) or slower (straight-line) depreciation method may be used. The selection of the depreciation method does not depend on what's happening to replacement costs of the company's fixed assets.

Many deplore this "looseness" or "elasticity" of accounting methods. In theory, one accounting method would seem the preferred or best method in particular circumstances. In other words, specific conditions would seem to lead to one and only one accounting method. So if two different businesses were in the same set of circumstances, their accounting methods would be the same. But in fact, their accounting methods might be different.

The authoritative pronouncements on GAAP over the years have narrowed down the range of acceptable methods, to be sure. But within this range there are still choices to be made. For an illustration, see Exhibit J on the next page.

The chief executive has to make certain that the company's financial statements stay within the bounds of fairness; that is, that the accounting choices are those in the range of GAAP. If the accounting methods are outside these limits, the financial statements will be false and misleading, and the manager will be liable for damages suffered by those debtholders and stock-holders who relied on the statements. If for no other reason than this, the manager should pay close attention to the choice of accounting methods used to prepare the company's financial statement numbers.

Once an accounting method is decided upon, the business must, for all practical purposes, stick with the method consistently year to year. So, if a business chooses a conservative set of accounting methods, its financial statements will continue to be conservative for many years.

Last, it should be mentioned that the real, or ultimate driving force behind the Income Statement numbers is the profit-making ability of management—making sales and controlling expenses. The choice of accounting methods makes a difference, to be sure, but only in a marginal sense, not in a fundamental sense.

Unacceptable Methods That Would Be too Conservative	Range of Acceptable Accounting Methods (choice of methods within this range are in conformity with generally accepted accounting principles)		Unacceptable Methods That Would Be too Liberal
	◄------------------- INCOME STATEMENT -------------------►		
—Arbitrarily charging off to expense now the cost of inventory that will not be sold until later	—Annual profit is measured as low as possible; sales revenue is recorded at lowest possible amounts, and expenses are recorded at highest possible amounts.	—Annual profit is measured as high as possible; sales revenue is recorded at highest possible amounts, and expenses are recorded at lowest possible amounts.	—Not writing off the cost of unsalable inventory
—Charging to expense now the cost of a major long-lived asset that will be used for several more years			—Depreciation of a long-lived asset over a much longer period than it will be useful to the business
	◄------------------- BALANCE SHEET -------------------►		
—Recording expenses for vague and nonspecific contingency losses that probably will not happen	—Assets are recorded as low as possible because expenses are charged out at highest amounts or at earliest time, and thus the assets involved contain the smallest cost residuals.	—Assets are recorded as high as possible because expenses are charged out at lowest amounts or at latest time and thus the assets involved contain the largest cost residuals.	—Failure to recognize the impending loss from lawsuits or other assessments the business will have to pay.
—Delaying the recording of sales that have been made in the ordinary course of business	—Certain liabilities are recorded at highest amounts because the expenses involving these liabilities are recorded at the largest amounts possible.	—Certain liabilities are recorded at lowest amounts because the expenses involving the liabilities are recorded at the lowest amounts possible.	—Recording sales before the sales are final, or failure to recognize the likelihood of large returns of products or large bad debts.

Note: Cash flows are not affected by the choice of accounting methods, except that methods used for income tax will affect the income tax payments during the year.

Managers Should Manipulate the Numbers

Business managers may try to avoid getting involved in choosing accounting methods. But this is a mistake. First, there is the risk that the financial statements may not be prepared according to GAAP in one or more respects. Using CPAs to audit the financial statements minimizes the risk of releasing misleading statements. However, even financial statements that have been audited by very respectable CPA firms have been found deficient; managers and CPAs have been found guilty in court trials, and they have had to pay large damages to debtholders and stockholders. Managers certainly have to keep aware of the consequences of reporting misleading financial statements. But there is a more important reason for managers getting involved in making accounting choices.

The business manager should decide which accounting methods best fit the general policies and philosophy of the business. In other words, the manager has to decide which "look" of the financial statements is in the best interests of the company. Putting it more crudely, managers can and should manipulate the profit numbers and the asset and liability numbers that are reported in their financial statements.

The point is this: the numbers have to be manipulated—if not by the managers, then by their accountants. By staying out of the decision making, the manager allows the accountant to do the manipulating. But the accountant may not be fully aware of all the policies of the company and the various pressures on the business. The manager may, given all the pressures and problems at the present time, need a rather "aggressive" set of financial statements, say to persuade the bank to make a loan or to convince a major customer of the financial ability of the company to carry through on a major deal or a long-term contract. But the accountant may choose conservative accounting methods instead.

The managers should select those accounting methods that best advance the interests of the business. The manager should ask whether the accounting methods of the business should be on the conservative end, in the middle, or on the liberal end of the range of generally accepted methods. These are not easy decisions. But the decisions are too important to leave to accountants alone. And, in the process of getting involved, the manager will certainly develop a much better understanding of financial statements, which helps in analyzing profit performance and financial position and in "talking" the financial statements when borrowing money or when raising equity capital.

Are Investors Fooled by Accounting Methods?

Like it or not, we live in a world of alternative accounting methods. Choices have to be made. Thus, financial statements are flexible. The financial statements for a business can be presented in a "small, medium, or large size," depending on which specific accounting methods managers select for profit accounting. GAAP permit this elasticity in the numbers reported in financial statements.

Management must disclose in footnotes which accounting methods have been selected to prepare their financial statements (see Chapter 17). So, investors can determine whether the business is being conservative or not so conservative in reporting its net income and financial condition. There is a fair amount of evidence, based on research studies, that investors make allowances for different accounting methods when comparing different companies. Also, studies show that when a company changes its accounting methods there is not a knee-jerk reaction to the new numbers reported by the company. Market value tends to remain the same, other things being the same. In short, investors are not fooled by the arbitrary selection or change of accounting methods by companies.

The overall conservatism of the financial statements of a business depends on two accounting methods in particular—the method to measure Cost of Goods Sold Expense and the depreciation method. To be sure, other important accounting methods may have a large impact on profit accounting. But the Cost of Goods Sold Expense method and the depreciation method set the tone for most businesses. Chapters 21 and 22 examine these two important benchmark accounting methods. First, however, in the next chapter we take a hard look at the recent fundamental change in accounting for the costs of post-retirement employee health and medical benefits.

20

MAKING AND CHANGING THE RULES

Why the Rules Are So Important

Virtually millions of persons depend on financial statements for crucial information about profit (or loss), financial condition, and cash flow of business enterprises. This sweeping congregation includes bankers deciding whether or not to make loans to business firms; investors deciding whether to buy, hold, or sell securities of public corporations; buyers and sellers of businesses deciding how much the companies are worth; owners of closely held businesses evaluating how the ventures are doing; suppliers deciding whether or not to sell to businesses on credit; and pension trustees deciding how to carry out their fiduciary responsibility to retired employees participating in the plans.

For that matter, what about business managers themselves? Keep in mind that managers are the first and most immediate users of financial statements. Managers depend on their financial statements to "know" how much profit was earned (or how much loss was suffered). And managers need balance sheet and cash flow information to keep on top of the financial condition of the business, to spot any solvency problems that may be developing, and to plan for the capital requirements of the business. In short, both insiders and outsiders need dependable financial statements that are designed for the needs and vital interests of all users.

Financial statements are the primary source and, for all practical purposes, the *only* source of profit and loss, financial condition, and cash flow information about a business.* It goes without saying that financial statements should be accurate, timely, clear, and complete. Financial statement users are primarily interested in the profit (or loss) performance and the solvency prospects of the business. The reliability of financial statements depends on two benchmarks: (1) how well profit is measured; and, (2) how well the financial statements reveal the solvency situation of the business. The financial statements

---

* This is not to overlook the fact that bankers, creditors, institutional investors, professional security analysts, and industry specialists spend a fair amount of time gathering information about businesses from sources other than their financial statements. And they spend a lot of time forecasting earnings. But financial statements are the only official source of information released by business entities. Even press releases by public corporations are subject to later confirmation in their financial reports.

contain other useful information as well, of course, but these are the two most critical reasons why people read financial statements.

This chapter looks at the rules that govern profit measurement and financial statement disclosure. Financial statements are no better than the rules followed to prepare the statements. As mentioned earlier in the book, these rules are called generally accepted accounting principles and include both accounting methods and disclosure practices. How good are the rules? Why are the rules changed from time to time?

We could logically conclude that the financial reporting system works pretty well, and therefore the rules are adequate to the purpose of financial statements. By and large the conventional wisdom supports this viewpoint. Nevertheless, this chapter takes a critical look at the rules. The remainder of the chapter is like a *Consumer Reports* test that gives a product fairly good overall marks (previous chapters) but then goes on to examine the shortcomings of the product and how the product could be better (this chapter).

Changing the Rules

As discussed in the previous chapter, financial accounting rules are a little "loose." Generally accepted accounting principles cut management a fair amount of slack. Managers can lay a heavy hand on the selection of profit accounting methods and they have a fair amount of discretion concerning what to disclose or not disclose in the external financial reports of the business. Clearly, managers know all sorts of information that is not divulged in their external financial reports and does not have to be according to the rules—more on this later. Our first concern is with how profit is measured.

External users of financial statements should keep in mind the "elasticity" of profit accounting methods, as discussed in the previous chapter. Managers can and do manipulate the timing of profit to some extent. I'd say that profit for any one year of most businesses could be at least ten percent higher or lower than the amount reported and still be within the boundaries of generally accepted accounting principles. On the other hand, there is one overriding rule that controls the manipulation of profit accounting methods, and that is *consistency*. Companies have to use the same profit measurement methods year to year or justify any changes. If they change, they have to report the impact of the change in their financial statements.

But are the rules themselves consistent over time? Financial accounting rules remind me of other rules, laws, principles, or standards that change over time. Remember when 55 miles per hour was the interstate highway speed limit? I grew up when there was no three-point shot in basketball. Roger Marris broke Babe Ruth's single season home run record, but Roger's season had more games. Likewise, financial accounting rules constantly evolve. Every year the Financial Accounting Standards Board, the authoritative rule-making body, introduces new rules and amends or repeals old rules. It wasn't that long ago, for example, that the Cash Flow Statement was not required and companies did not report it. I was a CPA for 13 years before earnings per share had to be calculated and disclosed in financial reports of public corporations.

Authoritative financial accounting rules lag instead of lead. First there is the problem; later a rule is adopted to deal with the problem. The usual sequence of events that lead up to the pronouncement of an accounting standard goes as follows: A profit accounting problem or a financial reporting disclosure issue develops in actual practice that is not specifically covered in the official rule book of generally accepted accounting principles. Criticism continues but actual accounting or disclosure practices do not respond.

Eventually the criticism coalesces into a sufficient consensus of concern that the Financial Accounting Standards Board puts the matter on its agenda. The issue works its way through the due process procedures of the board (which can take a fairly long time). Finally, a standard is issued. Often the new rule does not please all businesses. Nevertheless, business managers bite the bullet and implement the new rule, despite whatever objections they may have. Otherwise, their CPA auditor would object to their financial statements and the company would stand accused of issuing misleading financial statements.

Most financial reporting rule changes are very technical. The Financial Accounting Standards Board has issued more than 110 pronouncements since it started in 1973. If you took the time to look at the list of these rule changes I doubt if you would find very many of interest—although it should be said that corporate controllers, professional security analysts, and investment managers keep a close eye on all accounting rule changes. Most rule changes registered less than a 3.0 on a financial statement Richter scale—they caused barely a tremor in financial statements. But recently there was a rule change that caused earthquakes in the financial statements of many businesses.

This particular rule change is important for another reason, also. It serves as a sobering reminder of how established accounting and disclosure rules can be seriously deficient and remain so for a relatively long time before the accounting profession comes to grips with the problem. I don't want to overdramatize this particular rule change, but it does remind me of the title *Silent Spring*—Rachel Carson's famous book that exposed the environmental harm caused by many chemicals then in widespread use and the disposal practices that were generally accepted at the time.

A New Accounting Rule for an Old Problem:
Post Retirement Employee Health and Medical Benefits

One of the most remarkable developments in the workplace over the last generation has been the growth of employee health and medical care plans. Typically an employer pays a sizable share of the cost of these plans.* More and more businesses have sponsored comprehensive health and medical benefit plans for their employees—both during their working years *and during their retirement years*.

The business continues to pay part of the cost of health and medical benefits during their former employees' retirement years—until the employees and their spouses and other dependents die or otherwise lose their rights of participation. Financial setbacks have caused some companies to reduce

benefits or to shift more cost to their retirees. There have even been a few cases in which employers attempted to evade their legal and/or moral obligations under these plans. But by and large, businesses have tried to live up to their obligations.

In broad overview, a company pays for health and medical benefits during the 20 to 30 years an employee works for the business and then continues to pay for another 10, 15, or more years during retirement. The sum of these future costs for all the retired employees of a business can be a very sizable amount, to say the least. Keep in mind these are *future* costs, not costs that have to be paid out all at once at retirement. However, suppose a business did want to prepay all these future costs by putting aside an amount of money that would be kept invested until the costs were paid in the future. This amount is called the *present value* of the future stream of payments.

Think of the mortgage on your home. You could look at all the future payments you will make until the mortgage is paid off. Say you pay $1,000 a month and your loan has 20 years to go; the sum total of your future payments is $240,000. Suppose you win the lottery and want to pay off the mortgage today. You would not have to pay $240,000. If your mortgage

---

* As you probably know, most businesses provide many other employee benefits, such as retirement pension plans. Pension accounting has gone through its own controversial history of development and has more or less "settled down." It should be noted, however, that many businesses do not fully fund their pension obligations; typically a company lags behind in making cash contributions to the plan's trustee. This can become a very serious problem if the business gets into financial difficulties or goes into bankruptcy. The pension plan may not receive all the money needed to maintain full retirement payments to the participants. The same threat plagues post-retirement health and medical benefit plans.

interest rate is 8.0% per year you could pay off the mortgage for about $120,000; this is the current loan balance, or the present value of the future mortgage payments. Likewise, the present value of a company's future costs of health and medical benefits for its retired employees can be calculated.*

As a matter of fact, businesses do *not* put aside money. They do not actually pay over any money to a separate plan or trustee that would be invested until the costs are paid out in the future during the retirement years of employees. In essence, employees are paid in promises—promises that are enforceable but not exactly ironclad either. In short, employers have an accumulated unfunded liability for their post-retirement health and medical benefit costs.

Until recently, companies did not have to record this "creeping" liability during the working years of its employees. Companies did not load any post-retirement cost on top of the wages and fringe benefits costs paid during the working years of employees. No expense was recorded until costs were actually paid during the retirement years of employees. This delay in recording the expense and the failure to record any liability came under heavy criticism.

In late 1990, after some ten years of debate and deliberation, the Financial Accounting Standards Board mandated that businesses had to henceforth record post-retirement benefits costs *during the working years of employees.* Companies were given two alternative ways to make the accounting change under the new rule. The large majority decided to jump on the galloping horse and make a one time catch-up for all the years that the business had not recorded its post-retirement medical and health care costs. Staggering amounts of liabilities were put on the books with a one-time charge to expense.

A prime example is General Motors. Quoting from an article in the *New York Times* (National Edition, February 2, 1993, page C3):

> The $20.8 billion write-off is a 'catch-up' to recognize the total cumulative retiree health-care expenses for working and retired workers, as if the accounting standard had been in effect during the employee's working years.

An earlier article* reported other examples of amounts recorded for post-retirement medical and health benefits: Ford, $7.5 billion; AT & T, $5.5 to $7.5 billion; General Electric, $1.8 billion; Alcoa, $1.2 billion; and so on. These are huge amounts, to be sure, but keep in mind that the annual sales revenue of these companies are in the multi-billions. For example, IBM's pre-tax charge for its post-retirement benefits was $2.3 billion in 1992, the year it took the hit. Its sales revenue was $64.5 billion for the year. (For 1992 IBM reported a total loss of about $5 billion.)

---

* The future costs are difficult to estimate; the timing and amounts of these costs must be forecast many years into the future and are subject to several changes due to inflation in health care and medical costs and new types of treatments.

* The *New York Times*, National Edition, December 18, 1992, page C3.

Are the Rules Adequate?

One main lesson from the previous discussion is that accounting rules, as good as they are overall, have been sometimes slow in catching up with what's going on in the real world of business. CPA auditors cannot force management to use better profit accounting methods than are required by the established rules. Managers are under pressure to paint as good a picture as possible in their external financial statements.

If such poor accounting can go on for so long in one area, a natural question is to ask whether the established rules are deficient in other areas as well. Are there some ticking time bombs in the accounting going on in financial statements? Unfortunately, other serious problems come to mind.

I should make clear that the following observations are my personal views. Many may agree with the following comments. But there has not emerged any clamoring for rule changes comparable to what lead up to the adoption of the new accounting rule on post-retirement health care and medical benefits discussed in the previous section. Nevertheless, I think any serious user of financial statements should be aware of these shortcomings.

Many companies have major exposure for *product liability*. Unsafe products can lead to large lawsuits. You don't have to look any farther than the auto and drug industries to see this. As you would expect, businesses are very reluctant to record any liability for potential product liability until court proceedings have gone against them and judgments have been handed down. Of more remote concern, though certainly on the horizon, are *environmental liabilities* of manufacturing companies, public utilities, and extractive industries.

You should read carefully any footnotes in a financial report that refer to litigation action against the company. These footnotes often express management's opinion that no liability will be assessed against the company, but you should take this with a grain of salt.

There are other costs that businesses are very unwilling to record until the last minute—this general area includes *downsizing, restructuring, and extraordinary charges*. Examples of such costs are early retirement incentives to employees, shutting down or disposing of operating assets, and spinning off major segments of the business.

Declines in sales that go unreversed sooner or later lead to downsizing at considerable cost. Not until plans have been formally put into place is there any recording of the costs in financial statements. Furthermore, usually there is no warning of such impending actions in footnotes to the financial statements. Financial statement users have to rely on their own predictions about how a business will react to a sustained sales decline.

The problem of *asset impairment* always lurks in the background. On the one hand, a company should write off doubtful accounts receivable that probably will not be collected; likewise, inventory should be written down below original cost if certain products will not be sold or will have to be sold at less than cost. Beyond these two assets there is no general *mark to market* accounting rule for other assets. Businesses are loath to record loss of value in their assets until the assets are actually disposed of. Many attribute the savings and loan industry debacle to the refusal of most S&Ls to recognize the doubtful collectibility of their real estate loans.

For more than forty years there have been persistent calls for more disclosure in financial reports. The central logic of the 1933 and 1934 federal securities laws is full disclosure. But several items of information—clearly of interest and relevance to investors, creditors, and other users of financial reports—are not required to be disclosed in external financial statements according to established accounting rules.

Advertising and other marketing expenses do not have to be broken out separately in Income Statements, though they do have to be reported in a separate schedule in the annual 10-K form filed with the Securities & Exchange Commission (SEC). Maintenance and repair expenses can be used to manipulate profit year to year because these expenditures are very discretionary. However, these expenses do not have to be reported in Income Statements even though they have to be disclosed in the annual 10-K with the SEC.

Top management compensation does not have to be reported in Income Statements nor in footnotes. In contrast, this is a key item that must be disclosed in proxy statements of public corporations through which the board of directors of corporations solicit the votes of their stockholders. Also, a summary schedule or table of the stock share ownership in corporations does not have to be, and is hardly ever, disclosed in financial reports. Yet, the extent of institutional ownership of stock shares in a business, for one example, is of great interest to all investors and creditors.

Disclosure has improved over the years, to be sure. But in my opinion disclosure could still be improved without causing businesses any loss of their competitive advantages. Most organizations—religious, military, educational, and governmental—favor less rather than more communication. Business is no exception to this general practice.

Last, I would mention again what appears to be a growing incidence of fraudulent financial statements. This is not really a problem with the rules but rather enforcing and policing the rules. Many cases of high-level management fraud came to light during the late 1980s and early 1990s. Profit for one or more years had been deliberately overstated to the gain of the dishonest managers. Their techniques involved falsification and concealment of evidence. In virtually none of the cases did the CPA auditors discover the fraud, as discussed in Chapter 18 (see pages 105 and 106).

To think that all financial statements are pure as the fresh-driven snow is naive. People are people after all; we're not all angels. As my father-in-law puts it, "there's a little larceny in everyone's heart." But just because a few cops accept bribes doesn't mean all police are on the take. Clearly, the large majority of businesses prepare honest financial statements. But there are some crooks in business, and they are not above preparing false financial statements as part of their schemes.

Once these fraud cases were found out they made headlines and got much attention in the press, and deservedly so. Relative to more than 10,000 public-owned corporations in the U.S., the number of fraud cases per year is very small. Ideally, there should be none, of course. What is alarming is that the rate of incidence seems to be going up.

There are no easy solutions. All I can offer you is the obvious advice to be cautious. You should ask whether, given the nature of the business and economic conditions in general, a company's financial statements might not report all its liabilities or may overstate some of its assets. A healthy dose of skepticism is needed in reading financial reports.

21

THE COST OF GOODS SOLD CONUNDRUM

The Importance of This Accounting Decision: Introducing the Example

The cost of products sold to customers usually is a company's largest single expense, commonly being 60–70% of sales revenue. Gross margin and all the profit lines below gross margin are very sensitive to how the Cost of Goods (products) Sold Expense is measured. Clearly, managers have a high stake in how much profit is earned, so managers should understand how the biggest deduction against sales revenue is measured. As a matter of fact, the chief executive should make the accounting decision regarding which method shall be used by the business to measure its Cost of Goods Sold Expense.

Three basic methods are widely used to determine the Cost of Goods Sold Expense. All three methods have theoretical support, and all three methods are acceptable interpretations of the general accounting principle that cost of goods sold should be deducted against sales revenue in the same period to measure gross margin for the period.

A specific example is needed to demonstrate the accounting problem and to contrast the differences in profit and inventory values between the three methods. The starting point is *product cost*. For a manufacturer this is production cost; for a retailer this is purchase cost. A problem arises when product cost changes over time, when the next batch manufactured or the next batch purchased has a unit cost different from the one before. This is true for almost all businesses, of course!

Suppose a company sold 4,000 units of a product during the year. The company began the year with 1,000 units, which is the carryforward stock from the end of last year. Few companies would let their inventory level drop to zero. So, assume the company replaced products as they were sold during the year and ended the year with 1,000 units, the same quantity as its beginning inventory. To keep the example relatively easy to follow but fairly realistic at the same time, assume the company made four acquisitions of products during the year, each of 1,000 units. In short, the company replaced the units sold but did not increase or decrease its inventory level.

Exhibit K presents the facts of the example. Notice in particular that each successive acquisition cost $5,000 more than the one before. Now, before we proceed, I'd like to get your opinion on this accounting problem. How would you divide the total cost of the 5,000 units between the 4,000 units sold and the 1,000 units still on hand in inventory at year-end? (See Exhibit K again.)

EXHIBIT K—COST OF GOODS SOLD & INVENTORY EXAMPLE

Facts of Example and Questions

Batch	Quantity	Cost
Beginning Inventory	1,000 units	$100,000
First Acquisition	1,000	105,000
Second Acquisition	1,000	110,000
Third Acquisition	1,000	115,000
Fourth Acquisition	1,000	120,000
Totals	5,000 units	$550,000
Less: Goods Sold	4,000	???
Equals: Ending Inventory	1,000 units	???

I think you'd agree that the $550,000 total cost of the 5,000 units should be divided between the Cost of Goods Sold Expense for the 4,000 units sold during the year and the Inventory asset account at year-end for the 1,000 units not yet sold (but will be sold next year).

Suppose you are the chief executive of this company. How would you divide the cost? No fair sitting on the sidelines and letting the accountant decide how to do it. Too often managers simply go along with the method recommended by accountants without analyzing the situation for themselves. This is not a good idea. The choice is a management decision, which should be made like other management decisions: What are the alternatives? What are the consequences of each alternative? Which alternative is the best relative to the company's goals and other relevant criteria?

The Average Cost Method

My guess is that you would intuitively choose the *Average Cost Method*, as shown on this page. You would argue that $4/5$ of the goods were sold, so of $4/5$ the total cost should be charged to Cost of Goods Sold Expense, and $1/5$ should be allocated to ending Inventory. Put another way, the average cost per unit is $110.00 ($550,000/5,000 units = $110.00). This average cost is multiplied times the number of units sold to get the $440,000 Cost of Goods Sold Expense. The logic is that we are determining the gross margin for the whole year, so it makes sense to pool all costs for the year and then let each unit share and share alike, whether the unit was sold or is still in inventory at year-end.

However, the Average Cost Method runs a distant third in popularity. Much more likely the company would select one of two other methods, which are explained next.

EXHIBIT K—COST OF GOODS SOLD & INVENTORY EXAMPLE

Average Cost Method

Batch	Quantity	Cost
Beginning Inventory	1,000 units	$100,000
First Acquisition	1,000	105,000
Second Acquisition	1,000	110,000
Third Acquisition	1,000	115,000
Fourth Acquisition	1,000	120,000
Totals	5,000 units	$550,000
Less: Goods Sold	4,000	440,000
Equals: Ending Inventory	1,000 units	$110,000

The Last-In, First-Out (LIFO) Method

The last-in, first-out, or LIFO method, selects the four batches that were purchased during the year and charges this $450,000 total cost to expense (see Exhibit K, this page). The last-in, or most recent purchases are the first charged out to expense. Purchase costs increased during the year, so LIFO maximizes the Cost of Goods Sold Expense. The beginning inventory batch, in this example the $100,000 cost of inventory at the start of the year, remains as the cost of the ending inventory at the close of the year. The actual products on hand at the end of the year are those bought most recently. Nevertheless, LIFO allows the cost of ending inventory to be the residual batch left over after selecting the more recent batches to charge to expense for the year. Thus the LIFO method allocates to ending inventory the "old" $100,000 cost.

The primary theory of the LIFO method is that products sold have to be replaced to continue in business, and that the most recent (i.e., the last-in) costs are the closest to the costs of replacing the products sold. When there is cost inflation (as in this example), LIFO maximizes the Cost of Goods Sold Expense and thus minimizes the profit reported in the Income Statement. To do this, however, inventory is reported at the lowest cost in the Balance Sheet.

EXHIBIT K—COST OF GOODS SOLD & INVENTORY EXAMPLE

Last-In, First-Out (LIFO) Method

Batch	Quantity	Cost
Beginning Inventory	1,000 units	$100,000
First Acquisition	1,000	105,000
Second Acquisition	1,000	110,000
Third Acquisition	1,000	115,000
Fourth Acquisition	1,000	120,000
Totals	5,000 units	$550,000
Less: Goods Sold	4,000	450,000
Equals: Ending Inventory	1,000 units	$100,000

The First-In, First-Out (FIFO) Method

The reverse of the LIFO method is the first-in, first-out, or FIFO method. The FIFO method selects the beginning inventory batch and the first, second, and third acquisitions during the year, and charges this $430,000 total cost to expense (see Exhibit K, this page). The first batches in are the first batches to be charged out to expense. The $120,000 cost batch, being the last purchase during the year, becomes the cost of the ending inventory.

The primary theory of FIFO is that the actual flow of products usually is a first-in, first-out sequence. When there is cost inflation during the year (as in this example), FIFO minimizes the cost of goods sold expense and thus maximizes the profit reported in the Income Statement. And inventory is reported at the highest cost in the Balance Sheet.

EXHIBIT K—COST OF GOODS SOLD & INVENTORY EXAMPLE

First-In, First-Out (FIFO) Method

Batch	Quantity	Cost
Beginning Inventory	1,000	$100,000
First Acquisition	1,000	105,000
Second Acquisition	1,000	110,000
Third Acquisition	1,000	115,000
Fourth Acquisition	1,000	120,000
Totals	5,000 units	$550,000
Less: Goods Sold	4,000	430,000
Equals: Ending Inventory	1,000 units	$120,000

What Difference Does It Make?

In this example purchase costs increased 20% during the year, which is not necessarily realistic and which depends on the inflationary environment of business. LIFO results in $20,000 less reported gross margin compared with the FIFO method. In other words, LIFO gives a Cost of Goods Sold Expense that is $20,000 more than FIFO. Assume that total sales revenue from the 4,000 units sold during the year was $645,000 based on gross margin equal to $1/3$ of sales revenue, which is the experience of the company in this example. (The sales revenue amount is developed in more detail later in this chapter.) The $20,000 difference between LIFO and FIFO is about 3% of sales revenue.

And what about inventory? Ending inventory is reported at $100,000 cost by LIFO, compared to $120,000 cost by FIFO (see Exhibit K, pages 129 and 130). LIFO causes the asset to be reported at $1/6$ less cost than FIFO in the Balance sheet. This penalizes the current ratio, a key solvency ratio discussed in Chapter 23. The company's total current assets will look smaller compared with its total current liabilities.

In brief summary: during periods of rising costs, LIFO results in the lowest reported profit and the lowest reported inventory cost. Why, therefore, do companies use LIFO? One possible reason is conservatism. They want to err on the downside and not be accused of overstating profits or assets. Another possible reason for LIFO is to minimize profits that are subject to profit-sharing plans for employees or second-level managers, or bonus plans based on profits. Keeping reported profits low keeps the profit shares or bonuses low. Another reason might be to "hide" profits during periods of labor problems or union contract bargaining. Also, a company may need to make the argument that it needs to earn more profit and thus has to raise its sales prices.

Or, the main reason may be to minimize *taxable income*. LIFO is allowed for income tax purposes. LIFO reduces taxable income by $20,000 compared with FIFO, so the income tax bill for the year would be less. On the other hand, if corporate tax rates are predicted to go up in the near future, it might be better to use FIFO and declare higher taxable income now while tax rates are lower than they will be in the future.

Cash flow is important. A business may be in a very tight cash situation and need to hang on to every dollar as long as possible. Even if not strapped for cash, the business probably can put the tax savings to work and earn a return on its investment. Last, if inflation continues the business might as well delay paying its income taxes as long as possible and pay off in the cheaper dollars of the future.

LIFO Liquidation Gains: A Special Feature of LIFO

Once a business selects LIFO, it must remain consistent with it over the entire life cycle of the product. LIFO is a long-term commitment. (This is true for all accounting methods in most cases, as mentioned before.)

Furthermore, the business manager should think ahead about what happens in the last year of the product's life cycle. In the last year there is a *LIFO liquidation profit* that causes a rather large "blip" or one-time gain caused by selling out of the inventory. Refer again to Exhibit K on page 129. Now assume we are at a time five years later, and this product was phased out during this year. To simplify, assume that the company has kept its inventory at the same 1,000 units level.

During the last year, assume that the average cost of each purchase is $220,000, due to inflation every year since the year used in the example. Normally the company would make four purchases during the year and the total cost of these four purchases is charged to Cost of Goods Sold Expense by the LIFO method. But in the last year the company makes only three purchases and liquidates all its inventory of 1,000 units to provide the rest of its sales. This "old batch" causes the problem.

The cost of the old batch that is charged to Cost of Goods Sold Expense is $100,000, not the current prevailing purchase cost of $220,000. So there is a one-time nonrecurring gain of $120,000 in gross margin! And taxable income is also $120,000 higher as a result of the inventory liquidation.

All a business does by using LIFO is delay the reporting of a certain amount of profit, both in its annual Income Statements and its annual tax returns. Eventually, when the business reaches the end of the product's life cycle and liquidates its inventory, the profit that would have been recorded along the way by the FIFO method "catches up" with the business and has to be recorded.

Managers certainly should be aware of the eventual LIFO liquidation gain at the end of a product's life cycle. To go a step further on this point; the manager does not have to wait until the end of the life cycle. Instead, the manager could "force" this effect by deliberately allowing LIFO-based inventory to fall below normal levels. Toward the end of the year the manager could hold off purchases, thus causing the ending inventory quantity to fall to abnormally low levels. Or, a severe business downturn may force the business to drastically reduce its inventory levels and thus to dip into its old LIFO layers.

In short, the business has some potential profit in reserve, or on the shelf, in the form of inventory carried on the LIFO cost basis. There is nothing to prohibit management manipulation of reported profit by the partial liquidation of LIFO-based inventory. The manager can do this without any objection from the CPA auditing the financial statements, although such LIFO liquidation gains have to be reported in a footnote to the company's financial statements (if material).

Should the LIFO or FIFO Choice Be Consistent with Sales Pricing Policy?

Assume that you're the manager who sets sales prices for the product in the example. Needless to say, many factors and pressures affect sales prices. But to simplify somewhat, assume that normally you base your sales price on the most recent purchase cost and you let all the units in this batch go out at this sales price until you exhaust the batch. When you start selling from the next batch, you change your sales price based on the new cost of the next batch. As mentioned earlier, your sales price is based on a 50% markup on cost, which means that gross margin is $1/3$ of sales revenue. For example, if the purchase cost is $2.00, a $1.00 markup is added to get the $3.00 sales price.

Given these assumptions regarding sales pricing, your total sales revenue for the year is determined as follows (see original Exhibit K, page 127 for purchase costs):

Batch	Cost		50% Markup		Sales Revenue
Beginning Inventory	$100,000	+	$50,000	=	$150,000
First Acquisition	105,000	+	$52,500	=	157,500
Second Acquisition	110,000	+	55,000	=	165,000
Third Acquisition	115,000	+	57,500	=	172,500
Total Sales Revenue for the Year					$645,000

This schedule should make clear that you are following a first-in, first-out, or FIFO, sales price policy.

You should be very interested in the results that would be reported in your annual Income Statement by the LIFO and FIFO methods:

INCOME STATEMENT

	LIFO		FIFO	
	Amount	Percent	Amount	Percent
Sales Revenue	$645,000	100.0	$645,000	100.0
Cost of Goods Sold	450,000	69.8	430,000	66.7
Gross Margin	$195,000	30.2	$215,000	33.3

FIFO gives results consistent with your sales price policy: the Cost of Goods Sold Expense is exactly $2/3$ (66.7%) of sales revenue, and gross margin is exactly $1/3$ (33.3%) of sales revenue.

LIFO, on the other hand, reports that you are falling short of your gross margin goal. Managers, of course, rely on Income Statements for feedback on profit performance. The

LIFO method suggests that you should raise prices because your gross margin is only 30.2% of sales revenue. The LIFO method may be used to determine Cost of Goods Sold Expense. But this does not mean that the company is able to set its sales prices on the LIFO basis.

LIFO sales prices would be based on the *next* acquisition cost, i.e., the costs of replacing the units sold. In this example, the LIFO sales prices would be based on the four acquisitions shown in Exhibit K, page 129 ($105,000, $110,000, $115,000, and $120,000). This would require total sales revenue of $675,000, instead of $645,000, or $30,000 more sales revenue.

But could the higher prices have been charged to customers? Normally, competitive pressures keep sales prices down or delay the increase of sales prices. In short, a company's sales price policy may be "forced" by competitive pressures to stay on a FIFO basis. If costs of goods sold expense is on a LIFO basis, reported gross margin will be somewhat misleading. Managers definitely should keep this in mind when analyzing the gross margin performance numbers reported in their Income Statements. Likewise, creditors and investors should allow for this in evaluating a company's profit performance.

22

ACCELERATED OR STRAIGHT-LINE DEPRECIATION?

Long-Lived Assets as Capitalized Costs

When acquiring most long-lived assets, there are certain costs that could be put in asset accounts but don't necessarily have to be. In pure theory, these costs should be "capitalized," which means that the costs should be recorded in asset accounts and included in their total cost. As a practical matter, however, certain costs don't have to be capitalized.

For example, assume a business has just bought a new delivery truck. The purchase cost paid to the truck dealer has to be capitalized. Under the current income tax law, sales taxes must be included in the total cost of the truck.

The truck may be painted with the company's name, address, and logo. The business may put special racks or fittings in the truck. In theory, these additional costs should be capitalized and included in the asset account. But the costs are not directly a part of the purchase cost; the costs are, as a practical matter, detachable from the purchase cost.

Many long-lived asset acquisitions involve such additional detachable costs. New buildings certainly do. Beyond the basic contract price of a building the company usually has many additional moving-in and preparation costs. Likewise, in addition to the purchase cost of a new machine or a new piece of equipment, a business typically has installation costs.

Also, almost all businesses buy many tools such as hammers, power saws, drills, floor-cleaning machines, dollies, and so on. In theory the cost of these relatively low-cost tools should be capitalized if they will be used for more than one year.

For convenience the additional detachable costs associated with the acquisition of long-lived assets and the cost of small tools and like items will be called *gray area costs* in the following discussion.

Say a business has just purchased a new long-lived asset and has paid $50,000 cash for the asset. Shortly following the purchase the business incurs $5,000 additional gray area costs.

The $50,000 has to be capitalized and accordingly is put in an asset account. If not, the CPA auditors would certainly object, and the IRS could accuse the business of tax evasion. In other words, charging off the $50,000 to expense immediately is clearly in violation of generally accepted accounting principles (GAAP) and income tax laws. The $50,000 has to be allocated over the future years of use expected from the asset. Chapter 10 explains the basic theory of depreciation accounting.

On the other hand, the business manager could decide to allow the $5,000 of gray area costs to fall into expense this period. Instead of capitalizing the additional $5,000, this whole amount could be charged to expense this period. This penalizes this year's profits, but relieves the future years of this much additional depreciation expense.

Assume that the asset is depreciated over five years. Also assume that an equal amount of depreciation is charged to each year (just to simplify the example here). The impact on expenses for each year from the decision to capitalize versus not to capitalize the gray area costs is shown in Exhibit L on page 140.

Not to capitalize the gray area costs is very conservative. The first year's expenses absorb an extra $5,000, and the asset is reported at a lower cost value in the Balance Sheet. On the other hand, it must be remembered that in making this choice the company escapes a certain amount of depreciation expense in each future year. There is a "robbing Peter to pay Paul" effect. In the example above, year 1 is "robbed" by absorbing $4,000 additional expense, but years 2, 3, 4, and 5 are "paid" $1,000 additional profit. On the other hand, if the gray area costs are capitalized, each year is treated equally.

The main reason for not capitalizing gray area costs is to minimize taxable income in the first year (the year of acquiring long-lived assets). In the first year the amount paid out for taxes is lowered, and the company has the use of the tax saving until it has to be paid back in the future years. (Don't forget that taxable income in each of the future years is higher.) The cash flow advantage in the first year is very persuasive. This "free loan" from the government, plus the more conservative look of their financial statements, prevent many managers from capitalizing gray area costs.

Last, the policy of not capitalizing gray area costs and charging them entirely to expense in the first year provides business managers another way to manipulate reported profit. The timing of many of these expenditures is somewhat discretionary. Small tools can be replaced at the end of this year, or replacement can be delayed to the start of next year. Thus the expense can be held off until next year. Also, the acquisition of several assets can be delayed and "slipped over" to the following year. So the associated gray area costs would not be recorded as expense until next year. In reverse, the purchase of small tools and fixed assets can be speeded up, and thus the gray area costs would be recorded as expense this year instead of next year.

On the other hand, it can be argued that without any deliberate management manipulation the amount of gray area costs tends to be more or less the same year to year. So, there is something of a "washout" effect every year, and the net difference would be negligible. Indeed, for a mature business this may not be far off the mark.

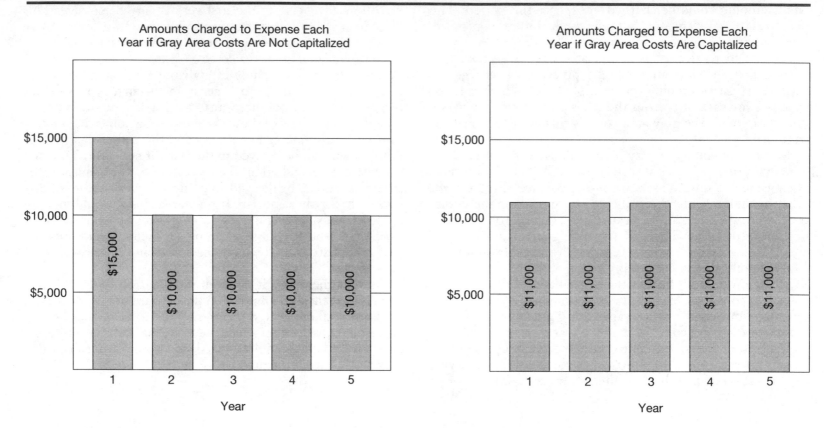

Amounts Charged to Expense Each
Year if Gray Area Costs Are Not Capitalized

Amounts Charged to Expense Each
Year if Gray Area Costs Are Capitalized

Deciding on Useful Life Estimates and Depreciation Methods

A building may stand 60 to 100 years. Yet the Internal Revenue Code (IRC) allows a 31.5-year depreciation life for tax purposes. An office desk may last 20 years, yet the IRC allows a 7-year life for this type of asset. And so on.

In short, the federal income tax permits long-lived assets to be depreciated over life spans that are too short, compared with the actual typical useful lives of the assets. This is a deliberate policy of the federal government, to encourage investment and to allow business to recover capital invested in assets over a shorter time span than the actual useful lives of the assets.

It's fair to say that the federal tax laws regarding depreciation lives have removed any attempt to be realistic in estimating the useful life spans of long-lived assets. In brief, the shortest allowed lives are adopted by the large majority of businesses. These "short lives" are found in the Accelerated Cost Recovery System (ACRS) now a part of our federal income tax laws. In fact, there's hardly any point arguing for more realistic (longer) life estimates.*

* However, the 1986 Tax Reform Act does permit assets to be depreciated over longer life spans.

All financial statement users should keep in mind that long-lived assets are depreciated too fast—not in the actual wearing out or economic sense, mind you, but in the accounting/recordkeeping sense. The reported book values of these assets in Balance Sheets are very conservative for this reason. This, plus the rapid pace of inflation, means that after a few years the total book value of a company's long-lived assets is far below the total current replacement cost of the assets.

Basically, a business has two alternatives regarding depreciation of its long-lived assets:

1. Adopt the income-tax approach, which uses short lives for the assets, and which also allows a front-end "loading" through accelerated depreciation; or,

2. Adopt more realistic (longer) useful life estimates for the assets and spread the annual depreciation over the useful life of each asset according to the *straight-line* method. The straight-line method simply means allocating an equal amount of depreciation to each (full) year of use of the asset.

For example, assume a business buys a new machine. The income tax law allows this asset to be depreciated over 7 years. Alternatively, the business may use a 12-year useful life estimate, which we'll assume to be realistic for this particular kind of machine. Exhibit M, on the next page, shows the difference in depreciation year by year, assuming the cost of the machine is $120,000.

Although accelerated depreciation has obvious income tax advantages, there are certain disadvantages. For one thing, the book (reported) values of long-lived assets are lower. (See Exhibit M again.) Some borrowing is done on the basis of these assets; mortgages or other liens may be given on the assets, or lenders may consider book values in their decisions.

The lower book values of its long-lived assets by using accelerated depreciation may lower the debt capacity of a business.

One final point: managers and investors are very interested in the growth (or decline) of profit year to year. Ideally, a profit increase this year over last year should be due to "real" causes such as better profit margins on sales, operating efficiency improvements, higher volumes, and so forth. Spurious increases in reported profit are misleading to managers and investors. Profit trends are difficult to track reliably if there are accounting "drop-offs" in annual depreciation expense, such as shown in Exhibit M by the accelerated method. The straight-line method has the advantage of keeping the depreciation expense constant year to year (on the same assets).

EXHIBIT M—ACCELERATED VERSUS STRAIGHT-LINE DEPRECIATION EXAMPLE

(Machine Cost = $120,000; Accelerated = 7 Years; Straight-Line = 12 Years)

Year	Accelerated Depreciation	Straight-Line Depreciation	Cumulative Difference in Book Value of Asset at Year-End
1	$ 17,148	$ 5,000	$12,148
2	29,388	10,000	31,536
3	20,988	10,000	42,524
4	14,988	10,000	47,512
5	10,716	10,000	48,228
6	10,704	10,000	48,932
7	10,716	10,000	49,648
8	5,352	10,000	45,000
9		10,000	35,000
10		10,000	25,000
11		10,000	15,000
12		10,000	5,000
13		5,000	0
Totals	$120,000	$120,000	

Note: Accelerated method based on Double-Declining Balance method with half-year convention and switch to Straight-Line method when advantageous; Straight-Line method based on half-year convention.

23

RATIOS FOR CREDITORS AND INVESTORS

When deciding whether to make or renew loans to businesses, bankers and other lenders direct their attention to particular financial statement ratios. Credit rating agencies, such as Dun & Bradstreet, compile financial statement ratios on thousands of businesses. The ratios provide a statistical profile of a business, for assessing its credit worthiness and the risk in extending credit to the business. If a company's ratios are weak, securing loans and trade credit becomes difficult.

Stock investors also focus on particular financial statement ratios. They are first concerned about whether the business will be able to pay its debts when they come due, as well as the overall liability situation of the business. Maintaining solvency (debt-paying ability) is essential for continuing operations, of course. Therefore, investors are interested in the same ratios as those looked at by creditors.

But investors have the strongest interest in the earnings performance of the business. They use certain key ratios to evaluate its profit track record.

This chapter briefly explains the basic financial statement ratios used by creditors and investors. These ratios are the

EXHIBIT N—BALANCE SHEET AT END OF MOST RECENT YEAR OF BUSINESS

(Modified Slightly to Show Total Liabilities)

Current Assets				**Current Liabilities**		
Cash		$ 256,663		Accounts Payable		$ 388,834
Accounts Receivable		578,754		Accrued Expenses		188,539
Inventory		978,094		Income Tax Payable		13,394
Prepaid Expenses		117,176		Short-Term Notes Payable		425,000
Total Current Assets		$1,930,687		Total Current Liabilities		$1,015,767
				Long-Term Notes Payable		$ 550,000
				Total Liabilities		$1,565,767
Property, Plant & Equipment						
Land, Building, Machines, Equipment and Furniture	$1,986.450			**Stockholders' Equity**		
Accumulated Depreciation	(452,140)	$1,534,310		Capital Stock	$ 725,000	
				Retained Earnings	1,174,230	$1,899,230
Total Assets		$3,464,997		Total Liabilities & Stockholders' Equity		$3,464,997

basic "scores" by which managers are judged by the suppliers of capital to the business.

The financial statements of the same company analyzed in the early chapters serve as the example in this chapter again. For convenience, the company's Balance Sheet at the end of its most recent year of business and its Income Statement for the year just ended are reproduced here—see Exhibit N, which we'll refer to often in this chapter.

Notice that the Cash Flow Statement for the year is not repeated. None of the ratios discussed in this chapter involve this statement, which may come as a surprise to you. Why not? Two reasons seem to explain this. First, the statement is designed to read as a whole and is limited to the sources and uses of cash during the year. Cash flow is vital, but not the complete story about the business.

Second, until fairly recently the Cash Flow Statement has not been included in external financial reports, so creditors and investors did not have this information readily available. There are virtually no standard or benchmark ratios for cash flow. Perhaps some cash flow ratios will emerge since the Cash Flow Statement is required in financial reports, but none have yet.

EXHIBIT N (CONTINUED)—INCOME STATEMENT FOR MOST RECENT YEAR

Sales Revenue	$6,019,040
Cost of Goods Sold Expense	3,912,376
Gross Margin	$2,106,664
Operating Expenses	1,523,288
Operating Earnings Before Depreciation	$ 583,376
Depreciation Expense	112,792
Operating Earnings	$ 470,584
Interest Expense	76,650
Earnings Before Income Tax	$ 393,934
Income Tax Expense	133,938
Net Income	$ 259, 996

Debt-Paying Ability (Solvency) Ratios

Always a key question is whether a business will be able to pay its liabilities when they come due. Failure to pay its debt on time damages the credit rating of the business, of course, and may jeopardize its very existence if the unpaid creditors take legal action to enforce collection. The sharp rise in business failures, including the bankruptcies of many well-known corporations during recent years, underscores the importance of keeping a close watch on the debt-paying ability of a business.

The Current Ratio: The Basic Test of Short-Term Solvency

One "classic" and widely used ratio to test the short-term debt-paying ability of a company is its *current ratio*, which is the company's total current assets divided by its total current liabilities. From the data in Exhibit N, the current ratio for the company is computed as follows:

$$\text{Current Ratio} = \frac{\text{Total Current Assets}}{\text{Total Current Liabilities}} = \frac{\$1,930,687}{\$1,015,767} = 1.90$$

The current ratio may be expressed as 1.90 to 1.00, but hardly ever as a percent (190%).

The general rule of thumb is that the current ratio should be 2 to 1 or higher. Most businesses find that a minimum 2 to 1 current ratio is applied by their creditors. In other words, short-term creditors generally limit the credit extended a business to $1/2$ or less of the company's short-term assets. Given this credit limit, a company's current assets will be twice or more its current liabilities.

Why do short-term creditors put such a limit on a business? One reason is to provide a safety cushion. A current ratio of 2 to 1 means there is $2 of cash or assets that will be converted into cash during the near future available to pay each dollar of current liabilities (which come due in the near future). Each dollar of short-term debt is "backed up" with two dollars of present cash or future near-term cash inflow. The "extra" dollar of current assets provides a nice margin of safety.

Theoretically, a company could remain solvent with a 1 to 1 current ratio. In this example, the three noninterest-bearing liabilities—Accounts Payable, Accrued Expenses, and Income Tax Payable—supply total credit equal to about 31% of total current assets. With this base of current liabilities, the company could conceivably convince bankers or other lenders to make short-term loans for the other 69% of current assets. But this would leave no safety margin for the lenders. Few, if any, short-term lenders would go this far out on a limb.

After all, creditors are not owners—they don't share in the net income earned by the business. The income on their loans is limited to the interest rates they charge. As a creditor they quite properly minimize their loan risks; as limited-income investors, they must.

In short, suppliers of short-term loans to business decide what the minimum current ratio will be, and usually they do not allow it to drop below 2 to 1.

However, the 2 to 1 ratio is only a rule of thumb; there are exceptions. Some companies such as car dealers can borrow almost 100% on their inventories, so their current liabilities are more than $1/2$ their current assets. Before accepting the 2 for 1 ratio for a business, it is a good idea to check the *average* current ratio for companies in the industry. For example, Dun & Bradstreet publishes the current ratio for a large number of industries. Motor vehicle dealers, as just mentioned, traditionally have carried on business with a 1.5 to 1.0 current ratio.

The Acid Test Ratio (or Quick Ratio)

Inventory is many weeks away from conversion into cash. Products are held two, three, or four months before sale. If the sale is made on credit, which is normal, there's another waiting period before the receivables are collected. In short, inventory is not nearly as liquid as Accounts Receivable; it takes a lot longer to convert Inventory into cash.

The *acid test ratio* excludes Inventory (and Prepaid Expenses also). The total of Cash, Marketable Securities (if any), and Accounts Receivable is divided by total current liabilities to compute the acid test ratio. It is also called the *quick ratio* because only cash and assets quickly convertible into cash are included in the ratio. In this example the company's acid test ratio is computed as follows:

$$\text{Acid Test Ratio} = \frac{\text{Cash} + \text{Accounts Receivable}}{\text{Total Current Liabilities}}$$

$$= \frac{\$256,663 + \$578,754}{\$1,015,767} = .82$$

The rule of thumb is that the acid test ratio should be 1 to 1 or higher, although you find many more exceptions to this rule of thumb than the 2 to 1 current ratio, such as in this example.

Debt to Equity Ratio

Some debt is good, but too much debt is dangerous. The debt to equity ratio is an indicator whether a company is using debt to its advantage, or perhaps going too far and is overburdened with debt.

For the company in this example (see Exhibit N), the debt to equity ratio is computed as follows:

$$\frac{\text{Debt/Equity}}{\text{Ratio}} = \frac{\text{Total Liabilities}}{\text{Total Stockholders' Equity}} = \frac{\$1,565,767}{\$1,899,230} = .82$$

In brief, the company is using $.82 of liabilities for every $1.00 of owners' (stockholders') equity in the business. Notice that *all* liabilities (noninterest as well as interest bearing, and both short-term and long-term) are included, and *all* stockholders' equity (paid-in capital plus retained earnings) is included in the debt to equity ratio.

This business, at a .82 to 1.00 debt to equity ratio, would be viewed as moderately leveraged. The company is taking fairly aggressive advantage of debt capital relative to its base of equity capital. Most businesses stay below a 1 to 1 debt to equity ratio, because they don't want to take on so much debt or because they can't convince creditors to loan them more than one-half of their assets. However, some industries are exceptions to this rule of thumb, and traditionally have had debt to equity ratios higher than 1 to 1, much higher in some lines of business and for financial institutions in particular.

Return on Investment Ratios: How Financial Leverage Helps (Usually)

Stock investors take the risk of whether the business can earn a profit and sustain its profit performance over the years. The value of their stock depends first and foremost on the profit-making record and potential of the business.

The basic test of a company's profit performance for its stockholders is not simply how much profit it earns, but rather how much profit is earned relative to how much stockholders' equity (capital) is being used to earn that profit. $100,000 annual net income relative to $250,000 stockholders' capital base is very good. $100,000 annual net income relative to $2,500,000 stockholders' capital base is very poor.

Dividing annual net income by total stockholders' equity gives the *return on equity (ROE)* ratio; for this company it is computed as follows:

$$\text{Return on Equity} = \frac{\text{Net Income}}{\text{Total Stockholders' Equity}} = \frac{\$259,996}{\$1,899,230} = 13.69\%$$

By most standards a 13.69% ROE would be judged pretty good. But, again, the ROE should be compared with industry-wide averages for the current year to get a true reading.

ROE is the bottom-line return on investment (ROI) ratio for stockholders. Bottom-line profit (net income) is divided by the stockholders' equity in the business. Other ROI ratios are also useful in analyzing a company's profit performance.

Another very important ROI ratio for profit analysis is the *return on assets* (ROA) ratio. The *before-tax* ROA ratio is Operating Earnings (before interest and income tax) divided by Total Assets; for this company it is computed as follows:

$$\text{Before-Tax Return on Assets} = \frac{\text{Operating Earnings Before Interest and Income Tax}}{\text{Total Assets}}$$

$$= \frac{\$470,584}{\$3,464,997} = 13.58\%$$

The before-tax ROA ratio tells us that the company earned more than 13¢ profit before interest and income tax on each dollar of assets used in the business.

The before-tax ROA is compared with the annual interest rate on borrowed funds. In this example the company's annual interest rate on its short-term and long-term debt is 8.4%.

The company can earn 13.58% on the money borrowed. So there is a favorable "spread" of 5.18% between the two. This difference between the two rates is the nub of *financial leverage*. Financial leverage means using debt capital on which a business can earn a higher before-tax ROA than the annual interest rate paid on the debt.

The total benefit from financial leverage can be computed fairly simply for a business. In this example the company has interest-bearing debt, as well as current liabilities on which no interest is paid. (This is true for almost all businesses, of course.) In total, all its liabilities supply $1,565,767 of the company's total assets (see Exhibit N on page 148).

The total cost for the use of this capital is the $76,650 interest expense for the year. Thus the company makes a sizable financial leverage gain on its liabilities, which is computed as follows:

Financial Leverage Gain for the Year

$1,565,767 (Total Liabilities)	×	13.58% (Before-Tax ROA)	=	$212,648	(Operating earnings before interest and income tax that is earned on the capital supplied by liabilities)
				− 76,650	(Interest expense)
				$135,998	(Financial leverage gain for year)

Financial leverage provided about $136,000 of the $393,934 earnings before income tax for the year, or about 35%

In a poor year a company's before-tax ROA may be less than its annual interest rate. In this situation financial leverage (on borrowed funds) works against the company. The high interest rates of the early 1980s combined with the severe slippage in before-tax ROA suffered by many businesses during this recessionary period provide ample proof of this point. The use of debt only aggravated an already bad situation for many corporations. Financial leverage cuts both ways, it should be remembered. The decline in interest rates in the early 1990s was a most welcomed relief to business.

Price/Earnings (P/E) Ratio

The stock shares of more than 10,000 corporations are traded in public markets such as the New York Stock Exchange. The day-to-day market value of these shares receives a great deal of attention, to say the least. Market value, more than anything else, depends on the earnings ability of the corporation. Therefore, market value is compared to net income (earnings after interest and income tax, or the final, bottom-line earnings of the corporation).

Because market value is per share, net income (earnings) has to be put on a per share basis. The basic idea of computing *earnings per share* (EPS) can be put as follows:

$$\text{Earnings per Share (EPS)} = \frac{\text{Net Income for Year}}{\text{Total Number of Stock Shares Participating in Net Income}}$$

EPS is not simple to compute, despite the relative simplicity of the concept. Many corporations use fairly complicated stock structures. They may issue preferred stock shares in addition to common stock shares. Their debt (and preferred stock) securities may be convertible into their common stock shares. Many other conditions affect the computation of the EPS.

In any case, once EPS is computed it is compared with the market price of the stock. The *price/earnings (P/E) ratio* is computed as follows:

$$\text{Price} \div \text{Earnings (P/E) Ratio} = \frac{\text{Current Market Price}}{\text{Earnings per Share}}$$

Suppose the stock shares were trading at $24.00 per share, and the corporation's EPS for the most recent year is $3.00. Thus its P/E ratio is 8.00. Like all the other ratios discussed in this chapter, the P/E ratio has to be compared against industry-wide and marketwide averages to tell if it's relatively high or low. Much depends on how stock investors forecast the future earnings prospects of the corporation.

The P/E ratio is so important that *The Wall Street Journal* includes it with other market trading information for all common stock shares reported in the New York Stock Exchange (NYSE)—Composite Transactions as well as the American Stock Exchange (Amex)—Composite Transactions.

The P/E ratio does not apply to private corporations, whose stock shares are not traded. The stock owners and managers of these companies judge profit (earnings) performance mainly by Return on Equity (ROE) and other return on investment ratios. One of their main concerns is how to maintain and improve ROE.

Last, it should be mentioned that EPS must be reported in the Income Statements of publicly owned corporations. This reporting requirement also provides evidence of just how important EPS is. In contrast, none of the other ratios discussed in this chapter *have to* be reported, although many companies do report their current ratios and return on asset and equity ratios.

Return on Equity: Final Comments

How can a business improve a poor ROE or maintain a good ROE? Three factors are key:

1. Financial leverage—keep the debt to equity ratio at the optimum level.

2. Sales revenue on assets—keep the sales to assets ratio as high as possible.

3. Control expenses—keep the expense to sales ratio as low as possible.

In brief, use debt to best advantage, make the best sales revenue use of assets, and keep expenses as low as possible. Each of these three key factors is discussed in turn.

The company in this example is at a debt to equity ratio of .82 (see page 149). As a practical matter the company probably couldn't increase this ratio too much. So not much improvement in its ROE can be made here.

Profit derives from sales. The higher the sales revenue from a particular set (given mix) of assets the better, unless the company sells at a loss. In this case the company's annual sales revenue is $6,019,040 compared with $3,464,997 total assets (see Exhibit N). Sales are 1.74 times assets; this key relationship is measured in the *asset turnover ratio*, which is computed as follows:

$$\text{Asset Turnover Ratio} = \frac{\text{Sales Revenue}}{\text{Total Assets}} = \frac{\$6,019,040}{\$3,464,997} = 1.74$$

If the company could squeeze out more sales from the same assets, its profit and thus its ROE should increase. The additional sales revenue should normally yield additional profit. Put in reverse, a decrease in the Asset Turnover Ratio will decrease the ROE.

Last, profit can be improved by reducing the ratio of expenses to sales revenue. Certainly every business should be cost conscious and continuously be on a program of cost containment and reduction. Its managers should ruthlessly examine every dollar of expense. The Internal Revenue Service, of all persons, probably has the best approach. The IRS demands two tests for any expense to be deductible—the expense must be *necessary* and must be *reasonable* in amount. It's hard to think of better guidelines for business managers.

24

A FEW PARTING COMMENTS

The Talk Behind This Chapter:
New Versus Used Stocks

Some years ago a local Woman's Investment Club invited me to their monthly meeting to talk about the meaning and uses of financial statements. It was a lot of fun, and it also forced me to rethink a few basic points. These women are a sophisticated group of investors who pool their monthly contributions and invest mainly in common stocks traded on the New York Stock Exchange. Several of their questions were incisive, although one point caught me quite by surprise.

As I recall at that time they were thinking of buying 100 common stock shares in General Electric. Two members presented their research on the company with the recommendation to buy the stock at the going market price. The discussion caused me to suspect that several of the members thought their money would go to GE for use in its operations. I pointed out that, no, the money would go to the seller of the stock shares, not to GE.

They were not clear on the fundamental difference between the *primary capital market* (the original issue of securities by corporations for money that flows directly into the coffers of the firms), which is entirely separate from the *secondary capital market* (in which present owners sell securities they already own to other investors, with no money going to the corporations that originally issued the securities). I compared this with the purchase of a new car in which money goes to GM, Ford, or Chrysler (through the dealer) versus the purchase of a used car in which the money goes to the previous owner.

We cleared up that point, although I think they were disappointed that GE would not get their money. Once I pointed out the distinction between the two capital markets they realized that while they were of the opinion that the going market value was a good price to buy at, the person on the other side of the trade must think it is a good price to *sell* at.

On other matters they asked very thoughtful questions. I would like to share these with you in this chapter, as well as a few other points that are important for anyone investing in stock and debt securities issued by corporations. These questions are also important when buying a business *as a whole*— for corporate raiders attempting hostile takeovers; corporate managers engineering a leveraged buyout of the business; one corporation taking over another; or an individual purchasing a closely-held business. Buyouts and takeovers bring up the business valuation question, which is discussed briefly.

Some Basic Questions & Answers

Investors in corporate stock and debt securities should know the answers to the following fundamental questions concerning financial statements. These questions are answered from the viewpoint of the typical individual investor, *not* an institutional investor or professional investment manager. My pension fund manages about $100 billion of investments. I assume its portfolio managers already know the answers to these questions. They'd better!

♦ Are financial statements reliable and trustworthy?

Yes, the vast majority of audited financial statements are presented fairly according to established standards, which are called generally accepted accounting principles. If not, the CPA auditor calls deviations or shortcomings to your attention. So, be sure to read the auditor's report. You should realize, however, that financial accounting standards are not static. Over time these profit measurement methods and disclosure practices change and evolve.

Accounting's rule-making authorities constantly monitor financial reporting practices and problem areas. They make changes when needed, especially to keep abreast of changes in business and financial practices, as well as developments in the broader political, legal, and economic world that business operates in. (See Chapter 20 for review.)

♦ Nevertheless, are some financial statements misleading and fraudulent?

Yes, unfortunately. The *Wall Street Journal* and the *New York Times*, for example, carry many stories of high-level management fraud—illegal payments, misuse of assets, and known losses were concealed; expenses were underrecorded; sales revenues were overrecorded or sales returns were not recorded; and financial distress symptoms were buried out of sight.

It is very difficult for CPA auditors to detect high-level management fraud that has been cleverly concealed or that involves a conspiracy among managers and other parties to the fraud. (See Chapter 18 for review.) Auditors are highly skilled professionals, and the rate of audit failures has been low. Sometimes, however, the auditors were lax in their duties and deserved to be sued—and were! CPA firms have paid out millions of dollars to defrauded investors and creditors.

There's always a small risk that the financial statements are, in fact, false or misleading. You would have legal recourse against the company's managers and its auditors once the fraud is found out, but this is not a happy situation. Almost certainly you'd still end up losing money, even after recovering some of your losses through legal action.

♦ **Is it worth your time as an individual investor to read carefully through the financial statements and also to compute ratios and make other interpretations?**

I doubt it. The Woman's Investment Club was very surprised by this answer, and I don't blame them. The conventional wisdom is that by diligent reading of financial statements you will discover under- or over-valued securities. But the evidence doesn't support this premise. Market prices reflect all publicly available information about a business, including the information in its latest quarterly and annual financial reports.

If you enjoy reading through financial statements, as I do, fine. It's a valuable learning experience. But don't expect to find out something that the market doesn't already know. It's very unlikely that you will find a nugget of information that has been overlooked by everyone else. Forget it; it's not worth your time as an investor. The same time would be better spent keeping up with current developments reported in the financial press.

♦ **Why should you read financial statements, then?**

To know what you are getting into, I would answer. Does the company have a lot of debt and a heavy interest load to carry? For that matter, is the company in bankruptcy or in a work-out situation? Has the company had a consistent earnings record over the last 5 to 10 years, or has its profit ridden a roller coaster over this time? Has the company consistently paid cash dividends for many years? Has the company issued more than one class of stock? Which stock are you buying, relative to any other classes?

You would obviously inspect a house before getting serious about buying it, to see if it has two stories, three or more bedrooms, a basement, its general appearance, and so on. Likewise, you should know the "financial architecture" of a business before putting your capital in its securities. Financial statements serve this "getting acquainted" purpose very well.

One basic stock investment strategy is to search through financial reports, or financial statement data stored in computer data bases, to find corporations that meet certain criteria; for example, whose market values are less than their book values, or whose cash and cash equivalent per share is more than a certain percent of their current market value, and so on. Whether or not these stocks end up beating the market is another matter. In any case, financial statements can be culled through to find whatever types of corporations you are looking for.

◆ Is there any one basic "litmus test" for a quick test on a company's financial performance?

Yes. I would suggest that you compute the percent increase (or decrease) in sales revenue this year compared with last year, and use this percent as the baseline for testing changes in bottom-line profit (net income) as well as the major operating assets of the business. Assume sales revenue increased 10% over last year. Did profit increase 10%? Did Accounts Receivable, Inventory, long-term operating assets increase 10%?

This is no more than a "quick and dirty" method, but it will point out major disparities. For instance, suppose Inventory jumped 50% even though sales revenue increased only 10%. This may signal a major management mistake; the overstock of inventory might lead to write-downs later. Management does *not* usually comment on such disparities in their financial reports. You'll have to find them yourself.

◆ Do conservative accounting methods cause conservative market values?

For publicly owned corporations that have active trading in their securities the general answer would seem to be no. Roughly half of businesses select conservative accounting methods to measure profit, which results in conservative book values for their assets and liabilities. Even conservative methods might cause opposite effects (i.e., higher earnings) in a particular year because of such things as LIFO liquidation gains in that year.

The evidence suggests that securities markets take into account differences in profit measurement methods between companies in determining stock market values. In other words, the market is not fooled by differences in accounting methods, even though earnings, assets, and liabilities are reported on different bases of accounting from company to company.

To be honest, this is not an easy general conclusion to prove. There are exceptions, but not on any consistent basis. Overall, differences in accounting methods seem to be adjusted for in the marketplace. For instance, a business could not simply switch its accounting methods to improve the market value of its stock shares. The market will not react this way; investors do not blindly follow accounting numbers.

There is one situation in which I would advise caution and careful attention to accounting methods—and this is when you are considering buying or making a major investment in a *privately held* business for which there is no market to establish values for the stock shares issued by the business.

◆ Do financial statements report the truth, the whole truth, and nothing but the truth?

There are really two separate questions here. One question concerns how truthful is profit accounting, which depends on a company's choice of accounting methods from the menu of generally accepted alternatives and how faithfully the methods are applied year in and year out. The other question concerns how honest and forthright is the disclosure in a company's financial report.

Profit should be faithful to the accounting methods adopted by the business to measure its profit. In other words, once the methods have been decided on, the business should apply the methods and let the chips fall where they may. However, there is convincing evidence that managers occasionally if not regularly intervene in the application of their profit accounting methods to produce more favorable results than would otherwise happen—something akin to the "thumb on the scale" approach.

This is done to "smooth" reported earnings, to balance out unwanted perturbations and oscillations in annual earnings. Investors seem to prefer a nice steady trend of earnings instead of fluctuations, and managers oblige. So, be warned that annual earnings probably are smoothed to some extent.

Disclosure in financial reports is quite another matter. The majority of companies are reluctant to lay bare all the facts. Bad news is usually suppressed or at least de-emphasized as long as possible. Clearly, there is a lack of candor and frank discussion in financial reports. Few companies are willing to wash their dirty linen in public by making full disclosure of their mistakes and difficulties in their financial reports.

There is a management analysis and discussion section in financial reports. But usually this is a fairly sanitized version of what happened during the year. The history of financial reporting disclosure practices, unfortunately, makes clear that until standard-setting authorities force specific disclosure standards on all companies, few make such disclosures voluntarily.

The disclosure of employee pension and retirement costs went through this pattern of inadequate reporting until, finally, the standard-setting bodies stepped in and required fuller disclosure. Until a standard was issued few companies reported a Cash Flow Statement, even though this statement had been asked for by security analysts since the 1950s! Recalls of unsafe products, pending law suits, and top management compensation are other examples of "reluctant reporting."

The masthead of the *New York Times* boasts "All the News That's Fit To Print." Don't expect this in financial reports, however.

◆ Does a financial report explain the basic profit-making strategy of the business?

Not really. In an ideal world, I would argue, a financial report should not only report how much profit (net income) was earned by the business and the amounts of revenue and expenses that generated this profit. The financial report should also provide a profit road map, or an earnings blueprint of the business. By this I mean that the financial report reader should be told the basic profit-making strategy of the business, including its most critical profit-making success factors.

In their annual financial reports publicly owned corporations are required to disclose their sales revenue and operating expenses by major segments (lines of business), which provides information about which product lines are more profitable than others. However, segments are very large conglomerate totals that span many different products. Segment disclosure was certainly a step in the right direction. For example, the breakdown between domestic versus international sales revenue and operating profit is very important for many businesses.

Businesses do not report the profit margins of their key product lines. Both security analysts and professional investment managers focus much attention on profit margins, but you don't find this information in financial reports. And you don't find any separation between fixed as opposed to variable expenses in Income Statements, which is essential for meaningful profit analysis.

If you were to study managerial accounting, you'd quickly learn that the first step is to go back to square one and recast the Income Statement into a management planning and decision-making structure which focuses on profit margins and cost behavior.

In short, the Income Statement you find in an external financial report is not what you would see if you were the president of the business. Profit information is considered very confidential, to be kept away not only from competitors but from the investors in the business as well.

◆ Do financial statements report the value of the business as a whole?

No. Its Balance Sheet does not report what the current value of a business should be on the auction block. Financial statements are prepared on the *going concern, historical cost* accounting basis—not on a *current market value* basis. Until there is a serious buyer or an actual takeover attempt it's anyone's guess how much a business would fetch. A buyer may be willing to pay much more than, or willing to pay only a fraction of the reported (book value) of the owners' equity reported in its most recent Balance Sheet.

The market value of a publicly owned corporation's stock shares is not tied to the book value of its stock shares. Market value, whether you are talking about a business as a whole or per share of a publicly owned corporation, is a negotiated price between a buyer and seller and depends on factors other than book value.

Generally speaking, there is no reason to estimate current replacement cost values for a company's assets and current settlement values of its liabilities.* Furthermore, even if this were done these values do not determine the market value of stock shares or the business as a whole.

The market value of a business as a whole or its stock shares depends mainly on its profit-making ability projected into the future. A buyer may be willing to pay ten times or more the annual net income of a closely owned, privately held business or ten times or more the latest earnings per share of publicly owned corporations. Investors keep a close watch on the price/earnings (P/E) ratios of stock shares issued by publicly owned corporations.

Also, it should be mentioned that earnings-based values are quite different than liquidation-based values for a business. Suppose a company is in bankruptcy proceedings or in a troubled debt workout situation. In this unhappy situation the claims of its debt securities and other liabilities dominate the value of its stock shares and owners' equity. Indeed, the stock shares may have no value in such cases.

◆ Should financial statements be taken at face value when buying a business?

No. The potential buyer of a business as a whole (or of the controlling interest in a business) should have in hand the latest financial statements of the company. The financial statements are the essential point of reference but no more than the point of departure for many questions. For example, are

---

* Exceptions to this general rule are when a value has to be put on the stock shares of privately owned business for estate tax purposes and in a divorce settlement.

book values good indicators of current market and replacement values of the company's assets?

Current values usually are close to book values for certain assets—marketable securities, accounts receivable, and FIFO-based inventory. On the other hand, book values of LIFO-based inventory, long-term operating assets depreciated by accelerated methods, and land purchased many years ago may be far below current market and replacement values.

Cash is usually a hard number, although a buyer should be aware that there may be some *window dressing*.* Every asset other than Cash presents potential valuation problems. For example, a business may not have written off all of its uncollectible accounts receivable. Some of its inventory may be unsalable, but not yet written down. Some of its fixed assets may be obsolete and in fact may have been placed on stand-by, yet these assets may still be on the books.

Some potential or contingent liabilities may not be recorded, such as lawsuits in progress. In short, the buyer may have to do some house cleaning on the assets and liabilities of the business, and then start negotiations on the basis of these adjusted amounts.

A potential buyer should also ask to see the internal management profit reports of the business, but management may be reluctant to provide this confidential information. For that matter, the business may not have a very good management reporting system that provides relevant decision-making and control information. The buyer can ask for information about product costs and sales prices to get a rough idea of profit margins. In short, the buyer needs both the external Income Statements of the business and additional internal management information.

A business might have certain valuable assets that the buyer wants for the purpose of selling them off, or the buyer may be planning radical changes in the financial structure of the business. There have been cases of a buyer paying less than the total of a company's cash and cash equivalents minus its liabilities. In other words, the buyer bought in for less than the immediate liquidation value of the business; this is very rare, of course.

---

* Window dressing refers to holding the books open a few days after the close of the year to record cash receipts as if the money had been received by the end of the year, to build up the Cash balance reported in its ending Balance Sheet. Unfortunately, this very questionable practice is tolerated by CPA auditors.

A Short Summary

You can rely on audited financial statements. The risk of fraudulent financial statements is minimal, although recently there have been several high profile cases in which large national and international CPA firms had to pay out millions of dollars to investors who relied on what turned out to be fraudulent financial statements. Overall, however, this risk is very small.

You might think twice before investing much time in analyzing the financial statements of corporations whose securities are publicly traded—because hundreds of other investors have done the same analysis and the chance of you finding out something that no one else has yet discovered is nil. On the other hand, for a quick benchmark test you might compare the percent change in the company's sale revenue over last year with the percent changes in its net income and operating assets. Major disparities are worth a look.

Reading financial statements is the best way of getting acquainted with the financial structure of a business that you're thinking of investing in. Don't worry too much about businesses that use conservative accounting methods. There

seems to be no adverse effect on the market value of their stock shares. For privately owned companies, on the other hand, you should keep an eye on the major accounting policies of the business and how these accounting methods impact on reported earnings and asset values.

Disclosure in financial statements leaves a lot to be desired. Don't look for a road map of the profit strategy of a business in its financial reports. Finally, the total value of a business is not to be found in its Balance Sheet. Until an actual buyer of a business makes a serious offer, there is no particular reason to determine the value of the business as a going concern. Value would depend most importantly on the past earnings record of the business as forecast into the future.

The main message of this final chapter is to be prudent and careful in making decisions based on financial statements. Many investors and managers don't seem to be fully aware of the limitations of financial statements. Used intelligently, financial reports are the indispensable starting point for management and investment decisions. I hope my book helps you make better decisions. Good luck, and be careful out there.